HUMAN CHATTEL—BOUGHT AND SOLD

Black men were not the only slaves in bondage to America's white men. Most Americans know little about the lucrative slave trade of Red Men that occurred in this country's Southwest from the 1800's up to 1935. When New Mexican slave raiders captured Indian natives, or offered various goods to marauding bands of Indians for their human captives, they helped keep the tribes of the Southwest at a red-hot pitch of hostility and intensified their conflict with the Government of the United States. Americans who read this disturbing report will learn about one of the most shocking and little-known chapters of their history.

To Matthew—

Introduction

Credit must be given to Christopher Columbus for not only planting the seeds of Spanish culture in the New World, but also for imposing upon the aborigines a European system of slave labor. On his second voyage, the explorer and his followers subdued the inhabitants of Española, and placed in bondage every Indian over the age of fourteen years. Within three decades the rigors of servitude and disease had decimated the natives of that Caribbean island—and in an ever-widening arc, Spanish slave raiders had to extend their search. Arawaks from the Bahamas and the Venezuela coast, Caribs of the Lesser Antilles, Huastec and Totomac from the east coast of Mexico, were procured for the gold mines and cotton fields of Española.

Wherever the Spanish went, the results were always the same—within a few short decades the indigenous populations melted away. The onslaughts of forced labor, European disasters, inhuman treatment by cruel overseers were all reasons for the wholesale reduction of Indians of the circum-Caribbean region. In an excellent study, *Indian Labor in the Spanish Colonies,* Ruth K. Barber points out that "the Spaniards came for gold, the Kings demanded tribute, and the class of colonists who came to the Indies could not or would not work with their hands; therefore, Indian labor was necessary for the very existence of the colonies." In short, the forced labor which the Spanish imposed upon the Indians was a product of tradition, produced with the meeting of two mainstreams of culture—medieval Christian and Moslem.

The late medieval combination of rising national spirit mingled with religious militancy to produce in Europe an atmosphere for a thriving slave trade. In 1452 Pope Nicholas V empowered the King of Portugal to sell into slavery all heathens and "foes of Christ," in that case all Moslems. Subsequent Popes and Catholic monarchs broadly interpreted this concept of the "foes of Christ," applying it to all captives taken during religious wars. In fact, slavery usually awaited anyone convicted of conspiracy, treason, soothsaying, and even wife abduction—as well as to all falling into the rather broad category of the "unconverted."

The Iberian peninsula was the point at which Christian slavery mingled and fused with concepts of Moslem servitude. The eastern practices of retaining household slaves, debitor servitude, as well as a generally humane outlook toward the lot of slaves, greatly modified Christian practices. Thus the Spaniards brought to the New World a tradition of slave labor that originated in two cultures—Christian and Moslem; and it was a natural consequence that the heathens there would be considered the "foes of Christ," and treated accordingly.

The vehicles which first marshaled the labor force of the New World—and sustained the Spanish—were the *encomienda* and *repartimiento* systems. While in the strict sense of the word these two systems cannot be defined as true slavery, they nevertheless aided the practice of enslaving the natives; and added greatly to

8

the misery of the Indians. Basically the *encomienda* system was nothing more than the allotting of Indians to settlers, who were deemed loyal and well deserving by the Spanish monarch or his representatives. The *encomiendero* was entrusted for life and the life of one heir, all the Indians inhabiting a certain region. From these natives were exacted tribute; and in turn they received care, protection, and education in "spiritual and temporal matters." In theory the *encomienda* system was conceived to be beneficial—its motives being not only economic but also religious. As a result of careless administration by royal officials, however, grave abuses were soon heaped upon the Indians. The amount of tribute grew in proportion to the decreasing number of natives—and this continued to such an extent as to virtually cause the extinction of the aborigines of the Indies and elsewhere in the Spanish colonies. Thus the word *encomienda* has come to be almost synonymous with slave labor.

Throughout most of Spain's colonies, the words *encomienda* and *repartimiento* meant the same thing. In Mexico, however, a special meaning was attached to the latter. There *repartimiento* came to mean a weekly allotment of Indians. For agriculture an Indian village was forced to contribute workers for twenty weeks a year, in apportionment of ten Indians per one hundred. With discovery of rich mining lodes this allotment was altered to four per hundred for mine labor—and it was the recruitment of mine labor which drastically changed the picture of Indian servitude.

By 1600 Mexico had emerged as a vital colonial possession. Discovery and exploitation of silver lodes created the incentive for the Spanish drive northward. Rich deposits at Guanajuato, Zacatecas, and San Luis Potosí, and in the sierras of northern Sonora and Durango, poured forth their wealth. To maintain production, and to staff the farms and ranchos supplying the mines, the Spanish needed labor. At first, subjugated Indians from the Valley of Mexico were brought

9

north to fill work quotas. But when this supply dwindled, a substitute had to be found. The intractable, semi-nomadic tribes of the north offered solution to the problem of decreasing labor force. These were people who could never be Christianized and exploited as had other tribes, but they could be "reduced" to slave labor.

Roaming tribes of Mexico's central plateau—the Chichimecas—were the first to feel the impact of slave raiding. Ever northward did the tide of this insidious commerce sweep. Into the lands of the Guachichiles, Coahuilas, the Tepehuanes; and on toward the southern Pimas, Seris, Yaquis—on until slave raiders gazed across the Rio Grande, and wondered what resources tribes beyond offered. It was not long until Spanish captains were casting covetous glances at Indian groups that may have been Athapascan—the Apache-speaking peoples of today.

The development of Spain's mining frontier would eventually have a drastic effect upon various Apache-speaking peoples. As ethnohistorian, Jack D. Forbes, ably points out in his book, *Apache, Navaho and Spaniard,* "Spain's techniques of Indian relations established . . . from 1542 to 1600 were to determine in large part . . . methods used with the Apaches in subsequent years." The hostility with northern tribes—engendered by slave raiding—forced Spain to develop its own system of subjugating indigenous populations. Force of arms and sheer military might was the first approach. That technique, however, only inflamed aboriginal groups, and with Indians possessing horses, the system of application of fire and sword broke down completely. The method of literally bribing Indians to settle in closed communities, was next tried—and thus evolved the mission establishment. Even with creation of this unique frontier institution—which was successful in varying degrees depending upon the people who it administered to—it proved impossible to undo the damage already inflicted by slave raiding.

Indeed, the policy of slave raiding existed side-by-side with the missionary effort, and worked much to the detriment of the latter. From the beginning of the 18th Century until appearance of Anglo-Americans nearly a hundred and fifty years later, the slave raid would be one method for dealing with belligerent Indian groups. And this method would be incorporated in the universal policy of Spain, of pitting one tribe against another. In that way, Indian strength could be sapped, never to be combined, and turned—in all its potential force—against the Spaniards.

Trading rendezvous were soon to be established at all points contiguous to Spanish settlements and Indian country. Along the natural arteries of communication—the Pecos, Rio Grande, San Pedro, Santa Cruz, and Gila Valleys—traders met with Indians to barter for loot. Back to the towns of Santa Fe, Albuquerque, and Taos, as well as to a dozen lesser communities, flowed a steady stream of captives—whose fate would be determined by the temperament of purchasing households. The consequence of this evil commerce was keenly felt—and was far-reaching.

Tribes which had previously been weak now flexed their muscles, becoming forces to be reckoned with through trade in captives, for which they received in return guns, ammunition, and livestock. Other Indian groups—those bearing the brunt of slave raiding—were pushed from their traditional lands, onto and against still other Indian groups, or into closer contact with white men—and this oscillation produced flarings of warfare which kept the southwest in turmoil for generations.

Conflict arising from slave raiding did not end when the Anglo-Americans wrested control of the southwest away from Mexico. In fact, there is every reason to believe that the trade in chattel was at its height from 1846 to outbreak of the Civil War. Many American military commanders, like their Spanish and Mexican counterparts, either aided and abetted this nefarious

11

practice or closed their eyes to it. Militia companies, recruited during intense outbreaks of Indian depredations, were often reimbursed for their participation in a campaign by being permitted to retain all captives as personal property. And many petty politicians maintained their strength and popularity by pandering to the whims of slave procurers and traders, whose only aim was to keep Indian tribes at a red-hot pitch of hostility.

* * *

Without the aid of a number of individuals and institutions this book could never have been possible. To David M. Brugge and J. Lee Correll, ethnohistorians for the Navaho Tribe, goes a debt of gratitude. Both men allowed the author, over a period of several years, to comb the huge historical collection compiled for use in the Navaho Land Claims cases. Mr. Joseph F. Park, Curator of Western Americana, University of Arizona Library, kindly pointed out the location of important Spanish ecclesiastical documents, and made them available for research. Appreciation is also expressed to the staffs of the Southwest Museum, Los Angeles; the Arizona Pioneers' Historical Society, Tucson; and the New Mexico State Archives and Records Center, Santa Fe, for kindly guiding the author to important documents. Last but certainly not least, appreciation goes to John Ressler of the Museum of Northern Arizona, for his well executed maps.

L. R. BAILEY.

Carbondale, Illinois.

SECTION ONE

Plunder Trails Southward

I

Records of various New Mexican parishes reveal that during a fifty year period—from 1700 to 1760—nearly 800 Apaches were anointed with oil and holy water, and baptized into the Catholic faith. These were not willing converts. No missionaries had been at work among Apache bands. They were women and children, taken against their will by slave raiders, and distributed by lot among the captors. In accord with Catholic tradition, these individuals were baptized into Spanish families. Although they bore Spanish names, these Apaches would never be a part of the family of their captors. Their status remained that of menials and servants.[1]

In most ecclesiastical records the term *esclava,* or slave, was carefully avoided. Only neutral designations were applied to these menials, such as "of the house of," or the "servant of." The record, nevertheless, speaks for itself—a thriving trade in captives was being conducted by Spanish political leaders and military commanders. Up and down the Rio Grande Valley, from Taos to Chihuahua City and Janos went the human commodity. Down the San Pedro and Santa Cruz Valley in Sonora flowed a steady stream of Indian captives. And the baptismal records for parishes in Chihuahua and Sonora substantiate this fact. Numerous entries bearing the designation—*a nino de macion Apache*—are recorded in the documents from Janos, Bacoachi, Nacozori, and Arizpe. All these captives were under the age of eighteen—for older Indians were too set in their traits, and could never be trained as menials. Children were always tractable.[2]

From one parish to the next can be traced the routes of trade for this Indian slave commerce. Up the San Pedro, Altar, and Santa Cruz Valleys went the slaving expeditions—their destination the sierras of present-day eastern and central Arizona. Farther east, between the Rio Grande and the Pecos, was mountainous country in which other Apache groups ranged. Out of Spanish and Pueblo communities, lying along the Rio Grande, went slavers bound for those points. Always the expeditions returned—sometimes empty-handed, sometimes with "loot." In the latter case, the same traditional processes were applied to the captives: baptismal, hard work—and eventual assimilation into the mestizo population. Little wonder, therefore, that Apache vengeance mounted as years went by—until by the mid-1770s Sonora and Chihuahua were on the brink of ruin.

The story of the trade in Indian captives is an exceedingly difficult problem to unravel. Inseparably tied to Hispanic Indian policy, international rivalry for control of the trans-Mississippi west, as well as with both Spanish and Indian economics—this commerce had enormous scope and impact. By subtle courting of Indian allies, and using them to conduct slave raids against hostile groups, the Spanish were able to maintain their balance of power in a far-flung empire. The seeds that Hispanic officialdom planted, however, germinated into a commerce so vile that it kept animosities alive for generations—causing trouble for subsequent administrations of Mexico and the United States.

* * *

The specter of international rivalry hung like a cloud over New Mexico at the opening of the 18th Century, as France made her bid to wrest control of the trans-Mississippi west away from Spain. In a rapid descent of the Mississippi River LaSalle planted in 1686 an ill-fated colony upon the Texas coast—and shortly thereafter French traders were probing the Missouri country, leaving their wares and influence among Caddoan peoples of present-day Nebraska. By 1706 France was at the eastern flanks of the Rocky Mountains, impinging upon Apache groups in southern Colorado.[3]

With each passing year the French strengthened their position. By 1710 Canadians had thoroughly explored the Missouri River for some 300 or 400 leagues. Three years later St. Denis founded Natchitoches on the Red River, pushing a wedge from Louisiana-Illinois county toward Mexico. From two sources—Illinois and from posts along the Missouri—Plains tribes would be utilized by the French in their bid for Spanish territory. And in their gamble, the French, like their opponents, would go to great lengths to accomplish their goals.[4]

To their Indian allies—Wichitas, Pawnees, Kansas, Osage, as well as the Comanche, the latter beginning their southward drift, the French dispensed large quantities of trade guns, powder and shot. Along with each trading session came proddings to raid tribes under Spanish domination—the Puebloans, and a number of Apache groups. Viciously, were the cruelties of the latter peoples pointed out: Had not Navajos stolen Pawnee children,[5] and were not the Jicarilla and Puebloans hunting buffalo upon Wichita and Kansas domain? The French urged their allies to retaliate—raid New Mexico; and like the Spanish, French traders would barter for loot and captives.

The Faraone Apaches—kin to the present-day Mescaleros—ranged between the Rio Grande and the Pecos, beyond onto the Llano Estacado. Unlike their northern cousins, the Jicarilla near Taos, this group had long bedeviled the province of New Mexico with their hit-and-run tactics. Running off horses from Albuquerque, Taos, and carrying women and children into captivity at Pecos, and Picuris, the Faraones added greatly to the turmoil in the 18th Century. To the French, this Apache group appeared as implacable enemies of the Spanish—and this natural animosity could possibly be heightened by establishment of trade with them.

Using other tribes as intermediaries, the French rapidly pushed their sphere of influence toward the Faraones—adding to their deadliness through a trade in loot—loot taken from settlements of the Pecos and Rio Grande Valleys.

Spanish reaction to this threat came slowly; and at first disbelief was the only response in Santa Fe. Apache and Navajo war parties had long raided tribes residing in present-day Kansas and Nebraska; and reports from captives taken during these forays never gave any clues to foreign machinations. In 1697, however, reports of interlopers began to filter into New Mexico. When a large Navajo raiding force was ambushed and nearly annihilated by Pawnees—aided and armed by "men in red"—reaction came in shock proportion. Prospects of a coalition between the French and tribes along the Platte and Missouri Rivers would considerably upset the power balance—and the Spanish, with no more than a few thousand settlers, could lose their precarious foothold in New Mexico.⁶

Spanish policy would be altered to fit the potentially explosive situation—and this revamping of interests would create a vicious circle of Indian raiding. Indian groups, who in the past had plagued New Mexico, were now courted as allies—as Santa Fe officials desperately attempted to establish a buffer between New Mexico and the anticipated onslaught of French-armed Plains tribes. Prior to 1697 Spanish officials took a dim view of New Mexican Indians raiding plains people—and contrary to usual Hispanic practice, were even hesitant about purchasing the fruits of such expeditions. In 1694 the governor turned thumbs down to a Navajo offer of Pawnee captives; as a result the Navajos had put their prisoners to death. Prospects of Franco intervention, however, considerably changed the picture—and the Spanish would show little compunction about bartering for Pawnee women and children, and reducing them to slave labor. By 1706 Spanish officialdom in New Mexico had become prime outlets for slaves, horses, weapons, and all other forms of loot taken from the Pawnee, Wichita, Kansas, and other tribes along the Platte and Missouri Rivers.

Voluminous baptismal records—many in the Archdiocese of Santa Fe—have been carefully combed by ethnohistorians for clues indicating the extent and impact of 18th Century slave raiding. David M. Brugge and J. Lee Correll, working upon the Navajo land claims case, methodically tabulated Indian entries—and their findings reveal insight into the nature of the Spanish reaction to the French-inspired threat, as well as greatly clarifying the muddled economics of the slave commerce.[7] Like their European opponents, the Spanish sanctioned the practice of taking captives; and urged their more northern allies to counter the French thrust in every manner. And the conduct of slave raids against Caddoans was not the least point in Hispanic defense policy. Beginning in 1702 ecclesiastical records for the more northern Pueblos and towns of New Mexico—communities in closest proximity to French-armed tribes—are replete with Pawnee baptismals. Without a doubt Taos, San Juan, Nambe, Zia, Bernalillo, and Pecos served as spring-board for expeditions, as well as slave trading centers. It was at these communities that resident priests anointed and baptized the captives, giving them the name of Spanish households—very likely the households of commanding officers of the punitive expeditions.

Slave raiding at inception of the 18th Century—unlike a much later period—was anything but clandestine. That fact is not only borne out in ecclesiastical documents but by civil and military orders as well. In 1714-15 an elaborate campaign was launched against Faraone Apaches; and its commanding officer was carefully instructed by Governor Mogollon not to kill Apache women and children. If possible, they were to be captured and turned over to the governor—as his personal property.[8] Although this particular enterprise developed into nothing more than a fiasco, with no captives taken, the governor's orders nevertheless demonstrates the readiness of Spanish officials to take a hand in the slave commerce. Even if the 1714-15 Faraone campaign failed, other punitive expeditions were more successful, for a continual stream of captives flowed into Santa Fe and adjacent towns.

It is intriguing to speculate on the fate of these captives. Most remained in New Mexico as menials to more prosperous Spanish and Mestizo families—the baptismal records clearly indicate that. However, there did exist a lucrative trade between New Mexico and the mining centers of Chihuahua. The mines in the Parral district required labor in almost insatiable amounts—and "heathen Indians" were always welcomed. In 1716 a large number of Comanches were transported to Chihuahua as slave labor;[9] and there is little doubt that many Apaches from New Mexico and the Plains region to the east, met a similar fate.

*   *   *

Spanish-Franco rivalry died a natural death with a shift of European power balance, and by 1727 the threat to Spain's possessions in North America had passed. No sooner had one problem slipped by, however, than it was replaced by still another—that of defense against marauding Indian tribes, several of which owed their strength to the struggle between France and Spain over New Mexico. The Utes and Comanches— both related culturally and linguistically—began to flex their muscles in the early 18th Century, pushing Apache groups, such as the Jicarilla, Cuartelejo, and the forerunners of the Mescaleros in upon Spanish settlements, as well as against still other Athapascan peoples. This oscillation and its accompanying conflict for territory and economic advantages created chaos for over a hundred years. And in their endeavor to combat the resulting tide of depredations, the Spanish resorted to the policy they had utilized during the conflict with France. The trade in Indian captives did not cease with the relaxation of tension between France and Spain.

It became a policy of Spanish officials, as well as the "special providence of God"—as one priest stated—to keep Indian tribes hostile to one another. In so doing, aboriginal wrath could never be turned against Europeans. By sanctioning a system of slave trading, Hispanic officialdom sapped tribal strength and at the same time filled their larders through a commerce in plunder. The Spanish insidiously spun their web of intrigue; and Apaches were pushed into raiding Comanches, Utes subtly played against Navajos—just as Apaches and Puebloans had been pitted against Pawnees and Wichitas.

To better coordinate the diabolical work and to afford an easy outlet for loot, a rendezvous system was established. Taos, on the upper Rio Grande, became the nerve center of the trade. There, according to one eye-witness, Spanish politicos gathered everything possible for trade and bater with Apaches and the then southward-drifting Comanches—"in exchange for deer and buffalo hides, and what is saddest—in exchange for Indian slaves, men and women, small and large, a great multitude of both sexes . . . [which are] . . . the richest treasure for the governors, who gorge ⁺ʰem- selves first with the largest mouthfuls from the table . . ."

In comparison, the brutality of these trade fairs— which were the private ventures of the governing men of New Mexico—made the rendezvous of the grizzled mountain man seem tame. These "carnivals" would match the horrors of any slave market during the height of the Roman Empire, or indeed, any of those which made the Near East famous for its trade in chat- tel. Fray Pedro Serrano pointed, in broken prose, the finger of accusation—and sanguine is his depiction of what transpired at the early New Mexican fairs:

> . . . when these barbarians bring a certain number of Indian women to sell, among them many young maidens and girls, before delivering them to the Christians who buy them . . ., they deflower and corrupt them in the sight of innumerable assemblies of barbarians and Catholics . . ., without consider- ing anything but their unbridled lust and brutal shamelessness, and saying to those who buy them, with heathen impudence: 'Now you can take her— now she is good.'[10]

The continuation of slave trading as a method of playing one tribe against another deepened in economic importance, as it tied into almost symbiotic relationship with New Mexicans, such tribes as the Mescaleros, Ji- carillas, and later, the Utes and Comanches. Traders began to go far afield, to exchange commodities desired most by the Indians. What is pathetic, however, is the indication that New Mexican traders and slavers cared not where the source of the "loot" lay—so long as the captives were young enough not to resist the training in Spanish tradition. Pawnee, Wichita, and hostile Apaches were not the only candidates for enslavement. Spanish women and children—taken during raids far into interior Mexico were often carried back to upper Rio Grande towns—and there traded to their "own kith and kin." The policy of playing one tribe against another and its associated economics, offered Apaches a haven for their raids into Chihuahua, Sonora, and Durango, and an excellent outlet for the loot.

* * *

By 1700 dazzling riches and conversion of large indigenous populations were but faded dreams. The far north—from Durango to the Rocky Mountains—had been opened. To the Spanish officer who had participated in the initial penetration of this vast area, the illusion had long since vanished. He knew well the precarious existence by which he was ensnared. A thin line of mining and mission establishments, around which had grown concentrations of mestizo populations, were the only bulwarks against the ever lurking tribes who still resisted—the Seris, Yaquis, and certain western Apache groups.

By now the Spanish army in the far north was but a shade of its former self—the day of the *gran entrada* had long since passed. Only seemingly endless garrison duty and pursuit of Indian raiders were the promises of the future. Although officers grew lax in their discipline, they still clung to the desire for prestige and recompense which had existed in the past. The growing mining centers, and the ranches supplying them, needed labor in insatiable amounts. It was not difficult, therefore, to trump up charges to serve as excuses for plundering more nomadic Indian groups, such as the Apaches, Seris—and even the sedentary Pimas, if the former Indians were too fleet.

Corrupt officials engaged in ventures other than strictly military duty; and supplied their agricultural and mining enterprises with Indian slave labor. General Jacinto Fuens Saldaña, Captain Andrés Rezabol, the latter being commander of San Felipe in 1701; and the military commandant of Sonora, Gregorio Alvarez Tuñon y Quieros, made or authorized *entradas* against Apache bands during the first quarter of the 18th century—not for strictly military reasons, but solely for the purpose of supplying ranch and mine labor. Shortly thereafter, the entire length of the frontier, from the Gulf of California to the confluence of the Rio Grande and the Rio Conchos, was aflame with violence. Apaches—now well mounted—struck with vengeance deep into Sonora and Chihuahua. Spanish troops, aided by Opata and Pima auxiliaries retaliated in kind. During the autumn of 1748 forays were conducted against both Apaches and Seris—and for the next ten years the war was one of attrition, with military expeditions being made as far as the Gila River.[11]

These *entradas* did not yield the dividends which Spanish officers were used to; and complaints were loud—that the Apaches "had . . . no towns or crops to destroy, and no property to seize . . ." Only "a few women and children as captives were all that could be expected" from such military operations.[12] It was even debated whether or not it was worth warring against these Indians. Regardless of divergent opinions, Spanish military raids still penetrated sierras known to be Apache retreats. Utilizing Indian auxiliaries, Spanish forces hunted down Apache bands—with little regard as to whether they were peaceful or hostile. During one raid from the Presidio of Tubac, in the Santa Cruz Valley, forty captives were taken, and distributed by lot to the troops and their Piman allies. Baptismal records also tell a tale which correlates well with military history.

Down the San Pedro and Santa Cruz Valleys in Sonora flowed a steady stream of Indian captives—taken for the most part by Piman allies. And the baptismal records for parishes in Chihuahua and Sonora substantiate this fact. Numerous entries bearing the designation—*"a nino[a] de nacíon Apache"*—are recorded in the documents from Janos, Bacoachi, Nacozori, and

Arizpe. All these captives were under the age of eighteen years, for older Indians were too set in their ways and traits, and could never be trained as menials. Children were always tractable.[13]

From one parish to the next can be traced the routes of trade for this Indian slave commerce. Up the San Pedro, Altar, and Santa Cruz Valleys went the slaving expeditions, all led by those "bulwarks of Apache aggression"—the Opatas and Pimas. Their destination were the sierras of eastern and central Arizona, where Apache camps existed. Little wonder, therefore, that Apache vengeance mounted as years went by—until by the mid-1770s Sonora and Chihuahua were on the brink of ruin.

The colonial government tried one measure after another to check the Indian depredations that were bringing death to hundreds of settlers, and desertion of settlements, mines, ranchos, and missions. The thin line of military establishments—the presidial system—which began at Fronteras, Sonora, on the west and extended to the Red River on the east—were totally ineffectual.[14] The Apaches had learned through experience to fight to survive—and they fought as assassins. Attacking only when success was assured, and then rapidly fading into mountain retreats before pursuit could be organized, the Apache warrior was unlike any Indian the Spanish had yet encountered. Apache mobility was a thing to be reckoned with. Inured to physical discomfort, this Indian could ride a horse to death—and, if he found no other, he dried and jerked its meat, and traveled on for another sixty or seventy miles afoot. No string of fortified sites would "overawe" these Indians. The Spanish, however, would go to great lengths in their endeavors to stop what in essence they had brought upon themselves.[15]

In 1765 the Crown sent a trusted minister, José de Gálvez, to investigate the turmoil on the northern frontier—and empowered him with authority to make sweeping revisions in Indian policy. It took but a short time for Gálvez to ascertain that Spanish arms would never be strong enough to subdue the Apaches. Upon weighing the effects of military campaigns and tactics, as well as all that was known at the time regarding Indian strength and movements, Gálvez concluded, "that the vanquishment of the heathen consists in obliging them to destroy one another . . ."

The policy formulated by Gálvez was nothing new—it had been utilized effectively since Cortez landed at Vera Cruz. But the military strength and precision of movement behind his tactics were unique to New Spain's far north. Swift, vigorous campaigns would be launched against all hostile bands. At the same time peace would be concluded with other tribes, as swell as with Apache bands—and they would be skillfully courted as allies against all hostile factions. Using the age-old technique of divide and conquer, tribes would be provoked into destroying one another. Added to this stratagem, the social and economic structure—in fact, the very core of Indian life-ways—would be undermined and eventually destroyed by establishment of a lethal commerce. Guns of inferior quality would be dispensed, as well as liquor; and tribes would be encouraged to raid one another. And the Spanish would reap the rewards in terms of loot and captives. In short, everything that was vile and corrupting would be unleashed against the Apaches—all in the hope that hostile groups could be turned against one another.

Although this policy yielded dividends, it nevertheless added impetus to a system and commerce that would spread chaos throughout the arid southwest until long after the advent of the Anglo-American period. With the crumbling of Spanish colonial power in Mexico, the trading centers, and policies and traditions which they followed, served not to bring peace—but created an incentive for Indian depredations.

A council was convened in 1767 to put into effect Gálvez proposals, and to study in detail a large scale plan of military reorganization. Five years later came the *Reglamento de Presidios,* which revamped the entire defenses along the northern frontier. Following upon the heels of the *reglamento* of 1772 came the formulation of what was thought to be an effective Apache policy. By application of unrelenting military pressure these Indians would be driven from their mountain habitats—forced into blind submission, and settled near presidios, where they would be under strict supervision. With usual tongue-in-cheek evasiveness, Spanish authorities noted "that this system does not aspire to the destruction or slavery of these savages, but . . . seeks their happiness by the most efficacious means . . ."[10] To the colonial administrators the "most efficacious means" was to place the Apaches in a *reduccion* program. There the Apaches would be bribed with gifts and plied with liquor, their social structure and value system would be undermined, until as a people they ceased to exist. Eventual assimilation into the mainstream of mestizo society was the goal of the Spanish—and this would be accomplished at any price.[11]

By 1786 all was ready to set this *reduccion* program into motion. Brigadier General Jacobo de Ugarte y Loyola took command of the presidial forces. From Chihuahua City and Arizpe, a pincer movement was launched against Indians hiding in the high cordillera separating Chihuahua and Sonora. A bonus for each Apache killed, and retention of all captives, spurred soldiers and Opata allies. By 1790 this policy of virtual extermination had yielded results; and directly contradicted the stated aims of Spanish officialdom.

The first clues as to the effectiveness of military movements are seen in the returns of captives. Beginning in the summer of 1785 large scale Apache baptismals were recorded. At Nacozori, Sonora, a dozen children were baptized, anointed, and placed with the families of returning troops. At the church in Arizpe, seven more captives were baptized for the same period. Unfortunately records for the next year are either incomplete or unreadable. But for 1787, the commanding officer of the garrison at Bacoachi, Captain Doncingo Venzara, served as *Padrino* for two males and one female Apaches—all under the age of twelve. This same officer acted in a similar capacity in 1778,[18] when he was godfather to four other Apache children.

During October and November 1788 a force of 280 "leather jackets" recruited from Bacoachi, Bavispe, Buenavista, together with 120 men from the presidios of Janos and San Buenaventura, marched against Apaches residing in the vicinity of the headwaters of the Gila River. The tangible fruits of this expedition were fifty-four killed and 125 captured.[19] None of the Apache captives ever saw their families or their homeland again, nor for that matter the projected reservation which the Spanish were establishing for the greater portion of the tribe. As these captives were women and children, their eventual destination were the homes of military officers and Sonoran politicos who had fostered the military expedition.

With threat of military chastisement and slave labor hanging over their heads as never before, various Apache bands submitted to the yoke of Spanish aggression; and settled in *Establecimientos de Paz* (Establishments of Peace). An estimated 6,000 Indians came down out of their mountain retreats.[20] Coyoteros from the Mogollon Rim settled near Bacoachi and Janos; Gileños from the east placed themselves, along with Mimbreños, at Janos and Carrizal. The Faraones, formerly residing between the Rio Grande and the Pecos, were settled at San Eleazario.[21]

In a concentration camp atmosphere, tribesmen were fed at an annual expense of 23,000 pesos. As with any relocation program, however, problems were immediate—problems which the Spanish were never able to cope with. Endowed with the understanding of the Inquisition, the Spanish had little insight into the vicissitudes of cultural reorientation. Not only were there dissenters among the settled Apaches who caused trouble, but large scale problems soon arose with local Indian groups, as well as with settlers—who feared and distrusted these Indians. Adequate rations were not always available, and ferment and revolt hung in the air. Regardless of these difficulties, the *Establecimientos de Paz* were successful to a greater or less extent, depending upon the forcefulness of the various commanders. The constant fear of bondage, however, kept the Indians in line the remainder of the century and into the next. The Apaches had momentarily been bought.

* * *

Mexico's struggle for independence, however, shattered political and military controls imposed upon the Apaches. During the 1820s one presidio after another was abandoned, or garrisons drastically reduced; and under this lax supervision Indians began slipping away to take to the plunder trail. Response to Apache raids again forced Mexican authorities to look to the northern frontier. Gálvez's plan would be tried again—but with modification. Forces in Sonora under command of Ramon Morales, and Chihuahuan military, led by José Joaquin Calvo, launched a joint drive to force these Indians once again into line. In 1831, at Santa Rita del Cobre, in southwestern New Mexico, another agreement was extracted from Apache headmen to remain at peace. For ease of administration, Apachería was divided into three zones. The Presidio at Janos would be headquarters for all Plains Apaches; Santa Rita would comprise the second, and administer to the Mimbreños and Gileños. The third would be the middle Gila, and include the bands constituting the Western Apaches. In contrast to past agreements, this time the Apaches would be forced to work for their subsistence. The day of the free handout had passed.[23]

Needless to say, this treaty was unrealistic—for no Apache would ever remain in one place for long, certainly not to work for subsistence. They were accustomed to ranging, residing in mountainous areas, and hunting and raiding in adjacent localities. Resentment over discontinuance of the rationing program initiated by Spanish authorities, ran high. It was no surprise when Mimbreños, under Juan José, arose in rebellion at Janos in January 1833. Other Apache bands followed suit, and the perimeter of Apachería spread southward nearly to the Tropic of Cancer.[24]

Failure of the 1831 treaty dismayed the people of northern Mexico. Few in number and widely scattered, they were unable to meet the threat—and Mexico City cared less about their "Siberia" to the north—for it was more expedient to look after political intrigue brewing in the national capital. Both Chihuahua and Sonora keenly felt the onslaughts of Coyotero and Mogollon Apaches, who moved quietly and swiftly down river valleys and over the plains to loot settlements, burn fields, and drive off herds and flocks—and in the fashion set by the Spanish—carry into captivity all the women and children they could lay hands on.

Never in history had the Apaches become such formidable adversaries, as after their revolt in 1831. A partial explanation lies in the fact, that they were now making fortuitous use of trading centers and policies established prior to 1772. Large quantities of muskets and powder, hauled overland from St. Louis by Anglo-American traders, filtered into trading centers located up and down the Rio Grande and Pecos Valleys, as well as throughout Texas. Cattle, mules, and horses by the thousands, and captives by the hundreds, flowed northward. Encouraged by their impunity, armed with superior weapons, and furnished a market for disposal of loot, the Apaches pillaged the farthest extremities of Sonora. In October 1833 a pitiful plea for public donations was issued by the governor to rise and arm militia to combat the raiders. Little, if any aid was forthcoming, and throughout the spring and summer the scourge continued unabated. Hundreds of citizens paid with their lives, scores of women and children were carried to Indian camps, or disposed of to New Mexican slave procurers. The north Mexican states faced economic ruin.[25]

In July 1834 the legislature of Sonora feebly decreed that the salaries of all government officials would be reduced one-third to meet increasing costs of troop maintenance and defense. In an effort to spur zeal in the militia, permission was granted to allow all who ventured out against Apaches to retain captured booty. Reduction of salaries produced more complaint than results—and citizen-soldiers pursuing Indians usually met ambush.[26]

As no treaties or recruitment of volunteer Indian fighters could check Apache depredations, Sonoran Governor, Escalante y Arvizu, on September 7, 1835, initiated the payment of bounties for Apache scalps. A reward of one hundred pesos was offered for the hair of any warrior, fourteen years of age or older—the plunder, including livestock and captives, could of course be retained by scalp hunters. Additional bounties of fifty pesos for scalps of Apache women, and twenty-five pesos for those of children under age fourteen, regardless of sex, soon followed.[27]

The bounty system committed the state to a policy of extermination, and compounded the Indian problem. But results came fast. On April 22, 1837, a Kentucky hatter named James Johnson, touched his cigar to the fuse of a concealed cannon loaded with scrap iron— and at close range fired into a band of unsuspecting Mimbreño Apaches. Thus, in the Sierra de las Animas of present-day Hidalgo County, New Mexico, the "vile industry of selling scalps" commenced.

As it had with James Johnson, the scalp bounty attracted men of every ilk. About the same time that this Kentuckian was lifting forelocks, a Scotch-Irish soldier of fortune, James Kirker, was organizing a party of Delawares, Shawnees, Mexicans, and Anglo-American mountain men, to castigate Apaches plaguing the copper mines at Santa Rita del Cobre. Scouting the valley of the upper Gila, Kirker soon subjugated the bothersome Indians—and his name was not long in becoming a terror to every Apache band.

Hearing of Kirker's good work, Governor José Joaquin Calvo of Chihuahua, invited the Scotchman to pursue his profession south of the Rio Grande. This time with a larger force—200 Anglo-Americans and Mexican adventurers, besides his Indian contingent—the scalp hunter went to harvesting hair in the summer of 1839—and with renewed vigor. For the next six years Kirker varied his activities from lifting Apache scalps to taking an occasional Mexican one— and a profitable harvest did he reap. In 1845 the now "Don Santiago," triumphantly entered Chihuahua City, with 182 scalps, eighteen captives, as well as a score of rescued Mexican women and children.[28]

Infuriated by the actions of men like Johnson and Kirker, Apaches only intensified their raiding. Between 1838 and 1845 the death toll steadily mounted, as peons were ambushed while tending their fields and herds, miners waylaid, and woodcutters scalped. So too, were scores of women and children kidnapped and carried northward to trade outlets, located along the Pecos and Rio Grande Valleys. So much did the populace of northern Mexico fear for their lives, that many settlements were abandoned. Arizpe's population dropped from 7,000 to 1,500, and that of Altar decreased by a third.[29]

Momentary relief from one enemy, however, was brought by the appearance of another. Outbreak of the Mexican war focused attention upon the northern frontier as never before. As Mexican forces marched toward Sonora and Chihuahua to meet invading "Gringos," the Apache menace became second nature— and upon termination of that conflict, Anglo-American occupation forces brought a measure of security to the country—however short lived it may have been. Withdrawal of United States military forces only signaled renewal of depredations by Apache and Comanche hordes.

* * *

1. Microfilm copies of parish records are on file in Special Collections Division, Library of the University of Arizona, Tucson.

2. *Ibid.*; also David M. Brugge, "Some Plains Indians in the Church Records of New Mexico," *Plains Anthropologist* (October 1965); pp. 181-189.

3. Alfred B. Thomas, *After Coronado: Spanish Exploration Northeast of New Mexico*, 1696-1727 (Norman: University of Oklahoma Press, 1935), pp. 12-14.

4. *Ibid.*

5. *Ibid.*, pp. 13-14.

6. *Ibid.*

7. Consult Brugge, *op. cit.*

8. Mogollon to Hurtado, August 26, 1715; in Thomas, *op. cit.*, p. 87.

9. Amado Chaves, *The Defeat of the Comanches in 1716* (Santa Fe: New Mexico Historical Society, 1906); also consult R. E. Twitchell, *The Spanish Archives of New Mexico* (Cedar Rapids: Torch Press, 1914), Vol. II, p. 184, item 279.

10. Report to Fray Pedro Serrano to Viceroy, 1716 in C. W. Hackett (ed.), *Historical Documents Relating to New Mexico etc.*, collected by A. F. and Fanny Bandelier (Washington: Carnegie Institute, 1937), Vol. III, p .487.

11. H. H. Bancroft, *History of the North Mexican States*, 1531-1800 (San Francisco: 1884, Vol. I, p. 516; also Peter M. Dunne (trans. & ed.), *Juan Balthasar Visitador to the Sonora Frontier 1744-1745* (Tucscon: 1957), pp. 19-20.

12. Bancroft, *ibid.*

13. Brugge, *op. cit.*; also parish records, Special Collections, University of Arizona.

14. The presidio system in the far north consisted of the following posts: In Sonora—Altar, Tubac, Terrenate, Fronteras; Chihuahuan establishments were Janos, San Buenaventura, Carrizal, San Elezario, El Principe, La Junta de los Rios Conchos y Norte, and San Carlos; San Saba, Babia, Aguaverde, Monclova, San Juan Butista del Grande, and Bejar at San Antonio, Texas, completed the line. See Alfred B. Thomas, *Teodoro de Croix and the Northern Frontier of New Spain*, 1776-1783 (Norman: University of Oklahoma, 1941), p. 48.

15. Spanish officers at the time were well aware of the source of conflict, and speculated upon it. IN 1796 Lieutenant Colonel

33

Don Antonio Cordero voiced his opinions respecting the cause of conflict between Apaches and Spanish: "Perhaps it was originated in former times by the trespasses, excesses and avarice of the colonists themselves who lived on the frontier exercising a subordinate authority." See Daniel S. Matson & Albert H. Schroeder, "Cordero's Description of the Apache—1796," *New Mexico Historical Review* (Vol. XXXIII, October 1957), p. 350.

16. *Ibid.*

17. Bancroft, *op. cit.,* p. 558.

18. Baptismal records for Nacozori and Bacoachi are included with those from Arizpe. Microfilm copy in University of Arizona Library, Tucson.

19. For details relative to this slave raiding expedition consult George P. Hammond (ed.), "The Zuniga Journal, Tucson to Santa Fe: The Opening of a Spanish Trade Route, 1788-1795," *New Mexico Historical Review* (Vol. VI, January 1931), pp. 40-65.

20. This figure is no doubt an exaggeration, for many Apache bands never came in. Instead, they retreated deeper into mountainous terrain and resisted Spanish might wherever possible. An expedition led by Jos. de Zuniga penetrated as far as Zuni, and encountered hostile Apaches in 1795. *Ibid.*; also Matson & Schroeder. *op. cit.,* pp. 352-53.

21. *Ibid.*

22. Francisco R. Almada, *Diccionario de Historia, Geografia y Biografia Sonorenses* (Chihuahua City: n.d.), pp. 72-73. For additional details relative to settlement of Apaches see Joseph F. Park, "The Apaches in Mexican-American Relations, 1848-1861," *Arizona and the West* (Vol. III, Summer 1961), pp. 132-134.

23. Almada, *Diccionario,* pp. 73-74.

24. *Ibid.*

25. Robert C. Stevens, "The Apache Menace in Sonora, 1831-1849," *Arizona and the West* (Vol. VI, Autumn 1964), pp. 215-216.

26. *Ibid.*

27. See Ralph Smith, "The Scalp Hunter in the Borderlands, 1835-1850," *Arizona and the West* (Vol. VI, Spring 1964), 5-6.

28. See *Ibid.*

29. *Ibid.*

II

On February 2, 1848, the Treaty of Guadalupe Hidalgo was consummated between the United States and Mexico, and the area comprising present-day Arizona and New Mexico passed into Anglo-American control. By virtue of this agreement the United States took on—overnight—the problems which had confronted, first Spain, and then Mexico—not the least of which involved Indian affairs.[1]

For generations military and political authorities tried in vain to cope with lightning-fast incursions of marauding bands residing to the north and east. Apache plunder trails crossed the present-day international boundary at half a dozen points. The western Coyotero Apaches had two roads which entered Sonora and bore along the Pacific slopes of the Sierra Madre Occidental. These trails, collectively labeled by Ralph Smith,[2] as the "great Stealing Road"—came out of the mountains of eastern Arizona, and passed over the Gila above San Carlos Lake. From that point the road —and literally it was that—for it was many feet wide in places—ran down Aravaipa Creek, turned southward across San Pedro Valley, passing what is today Bisbee, and finally entered Sonora, northwest of Fronteras. From that region, thick with ranchos, the trail branched—southwest to the ranchos and mines around Magdalena; southeast to the Opata villages of Bacoachi and Nacozori, or straight ahead to Hermosillo and Arizpe.

The eastern Coyotero road crossed the Gila farther up stream; and led along San Simon Creek, dropped through the deserted San Bernardino Rancho and penetrated the Sierra Madres, where it then branched toward both Chihuahua and Sonora.

Apaches from the Mogollon Rim and the White Mountains, on the western margins of New Mexico, utilized what Smith calls the "Copper Road." This trail, running from Santa Fe, New Mexico, to Chihuahua City, gave these Indians choice of three plunder areas: If followed across Chihuahua, the road intersected the El Paso del Notre-Chihuahua City road, above James Kirker's old headquarters at the great ranch of Encinillas. From there, Apaches raided all around the capital. The second Mogolloñero road branched off the Copper Road to the right, below Lake Playas and Animas Peak in southwest New Mexico, entering Sonora, to reach ranches and mines located from the Continental Divide to the Pacific Coast.

The third trail took off from the Copper Road above Janos in northwest Chihuahua, and veered to the right. Bearing along the Continental Divide to the Papigochic and Tomochic Rivers, this road funneled Apaches down upon Mexican and Tarahumara villages; and enabled them to strike at the bullion caravans coming from the rich Jesus Maria mines. Sometimes Mogoíloñeros fanned out southeastward and southward to the middle and upper Conchos and its tributaries, or pushed to the Durango border.

The Mescalero Apaches, residing in the mountains east of the Rio Grande, from the Sierra Blanca toward the Big Bend, passed into eastern Chihuahua by way of the Pass of El Morion, at Dolores, and made for the highlands between Gallegos and Agua Nueva, on the El Paso-Chihuahua City road. Farther to the east ran still another road—the great Comanche War Trail.

Across the Llano Estacado of west Texas, and into Chihuahua by way of Lajitas and Vado de Chisos, a well-beaten path delivered annually hordes of South Plains warriors—who rendezvoused in the mountains of the Bolson de Mapimi, of eastern Chihuahua and western Coahuila. There, other Comanche and Kiowas would gather for winter and spring raids—and the entire area between the Conchos River, the Gulf of Mexico, and the Tropic of Cancer, was methodically laid waste.[3]

* * *

Horses, mules, bullion and copper pots were not the only products flowing northward over these plunder trails. Pathetic stories of women and children dragged into captivity fill both Mexican and Anglo-American literature. A ready outlet existed for any Indian groups desiring to dispose of human loot. In common with Navajo, Paiute and other captive Indians, the gentry of the Rio Grande Valley, or the traders at Santa Fe, Bent's Fort and Taos purchased Mexicans taken captive five hundred miles below Paso del Norte.

The manner in which this commerce was aided and abetted by inhabitants of New Mexico is not only tragic, but shocking. Mules taken from ranchos of Sonora, Chihuahua, Durango, and Sinaloa were sold for twenty to thirty dollars per head in settlements up and down the Rio Grand.[4] But as fledging Anglo authorities were soon to find out—the real profit came not from livestock, but from the sale of captives—hundreds of which passed over the international boundary. "The value of captives," wrote James Calhoun, the first American Indian Agent in New Mexico, "depended upon age, sex, beauty and usefulness. Good looking females, not having passed the 'sear and yellow leaf' are valued from $50 to $150 each. Males, as they may be useful, one-half less, never more."[5]

Calhoun's estimates of going price for captives were based upon figures of final transaction. In short, upon retail price. By the time a captive reached the settlement and final destination, he or she might have passed through the hands of half a dozen intermediaries. What was given an Indian captor for his chattel was a different story—a story which must be viewed in terms of "trade goods," for captives were just that in New Mexico during the mid-1800s. The New Mexican slave procurers, who were the outlet for loot carried northward by marauding bands, offered their goods to gentry of the southwest at still a different price. Perhaps the clearest picture of what traders paid the Indian for Mexican captives is again given by Agent James Calhoun.

When this agent reported upon the condition of a number of freed captives, the Southerner did not use the picturesque tobacco auction language he had before. Instead he wrote tersely:

"Refugio Picaros, about twelve years of age, was taken from a rancho, called Papascal, near St. Jago, State of Durango, Mexico, two years ago by Comanches, who immediately sold him to the Apaches, and with them he lived and roamed . . . until January last (1850), when he was bought by Jos. Francisco Lucero, a Mexican residing at the Moro . . . He says, the purchase was made at the Cerro Carmel, about two days travel east from the Rio del Norte, and four knives, one plug of tobacco, two fanegas of corn, four blankets, and six yards of red Indian cloth, were paid for him.

"Teodora Martel, ten or twelve years of age, was taken from the service of José Alvardo at La Papes, near Saltillo, Mexico, by Apaches two years ago; and he remained the greater portion of the time on the west side of the Rio del Norte. He was bought by Powler Sandoval, who also resides at the Moro, from the Apaches at Agua Azul, near the Pecos River . . ., in February last. The payment for him was one mare, one rifle, one shirt, one pair of drawers, thirty small packages of powder, some bullets, and one buffalo robe. The *boy* was claimed by Diego Sandoval, from whom I received him.

"Caudalans Galope, about twelve years of age, was seized by the Apaches, he thinks four years ago, at the Rancho Fernandez, near Santa Cruz, Mexico. Two brothers and sisters of his were taken at the same time, and he supposes they are yet with the Apaches. His father and mother were alive at the time he was captured. He was bought from the Apaches in January or February last by Vincente Romero of the Moro, at a place called La Cerro Queso, perhaps 'El Cerro del Queso,' east of the Rio del Norte in this territory. Price paid was some corn and tobacco, one knife, one shirt, one mule, one small package of powder, and a few balls."

Rosalie Taveris, related Calhoun, was "about twenty-five years of age, resided in Monclova, and was captured in November last by a band of Apaches and Comanches, within two days' travel of Monclova. Her husband, Santiago Costellan, and her daughter, four years old, were killed at that time. Her mother, Etuedas Guerris, lives in Monclova. She (Rosalie) . . . was bought from the Apaches by Powler Sandoval . . . at Cerro Queso, January last . . ., for two striped blankets, ten yards blue cotton drilling, ten yards calicos, ten yards cotton shirting, two handkerchiefs, four plugs of tobacco, one bag of corn and one knife."

Because of her age, Rosalie Taveris was better able to relate circumstances of her captivity. The fate of less hardy captives, who could not stand the rigors of rapid travel, as well as the curel treatment administered by the Indians, struck a sympathetic chord in Calhoun's mind; and he wrote to the Commissioner of Indian Affairs in hope that the government would take measures to suppress the trade of captives.

"The band by whom she was captured consisted of about fifty Indians who seized at the same time eight other captives, strangers to her—and all but two, who sickened and died (perhaps killed) were brought from Mexico into this territory with her. She states there are a great number of captives at and near La Cerro Queso, that all the men who are captured are killed; that parties of Apaches and Comanches are constantly going and coming in with horses, mules, sheep, goats, cows, goods, money and captives . . ."[6]

What Calhoun gathered from interviews with Mexicans having been freed from Indian bondage, was true. There were specific rendezvous, where traders met returning war parties. The Sierra Guadalupe, between El Paso and San Antonio, was a terminus of the westernmost Comanche trail—and it was to that landmark that South Plains Indians, and their Apache cohorts, headed to dispose of contraband and loot to *Comancheros*— those itinerant traders from New Mexico.

March and April were rendezvous time; and the motley congregation to be found at these points was anything but small. In 1850 it was reported that as many as a thousand Apaches and Comanches were encamped about the Sierra Guadalupe—and they "were all well mounted on fine mules and horses," with upwards of fifty captives with them, all taken from Mexico . . ."[7]

Farther to the west, on the Pecos River, were the large cottonwood groves of Bosque Grande and Bosque Redondo, twenty-five miles to the north. These spots were the hubs from which arteries of trade radiated in four directions. From the south came returning Mescalero war parties. Comanches, Kiowas and Lipan Apaches came from the east; and Apaches from the Mogollon Rim to the west. There they met New Mexican traders from the north.

Mexican communities along the Pecos derived to a

large extent their livelihood from the Indian trade—and they acted as middleman in the slave commerce. Upper Anton Chico, a town of 500 population in 1850, and its sister town of Lower Anton Chico, were notorious for their dealings with Apaches and Comanches. Inhabitants of these hamlets repeatedly defied Anglo-American trade regulations, by not filing proper trade permits with the Superintendent of Indian Affairs, and by carrying on intercourse with tribes designated as "hostile."

Brevet Lieutenant Owen Chapman, of the First Dragoons, reported upon completion of a reconnaissance of the Pecos Valley in 1851, that residents of both towns "are more frequently in communication and on better terms with the Indians than all the other towns put together, whilst their remote position enables them to trade unlicensed with the savages. Upon the approach of any troops, the Indians are duly notified by their friends, the traders . . . Nothing but strong civil measures or the constant presence of a military force sufficient to put a stop to this illegal traffic will prevent the Indians from being coaxed into the settlements, traded out of all they possess and afterwards stealing from the herds to prevent starvation. The whisky sellers and the traders thrive while the agricultural people suffer."[8]

Indians returning from raids south of the border literally beat paths to the doors of these trade communities. For as Captain D. Chandler wrote, "following up the Pecos to Anton Chico are old well worn trails or roads, made by the Comanches. Frequently thirteen distinct paths were counted running parallel to each other and a few feet apart."[9]

Towns along the base of the Manzana Mountains, namely those of Tohupadera, Doña Ana and Manzana, also aided and abetted raiding Indians, principally Mescalero and Jicarilla Apaches. At the town of Limitar, south of Albuquerque, was headquarters for still another group of traders who kept Gila Apaches well supplied with guns, powder, shot, and liquor; and took from the Indians in return, mules and captives.[10] So lucrative was the commerce with Apache groups, that citizens of southern and central New Mexican communities adopted much the same attitude which northern communities had for the Navajos and Utes—or as one chronicler wrote, *"Bueno Apaches."*[11]

* * *

At inception of Anglo-American occupation in the southwest, the problem of controlling the activities of Indian traders was difficult. The terrain was mountainous and semi-arid; and into this region poured the riff-raff of two nations—Mexico and the United States. The uncordial relations existing between the two countries —a natural aftermath of war—made it easy for illicit traders to operate. Their clandestine activities would not only act as impetus for Indian raids deep into Mexico, but also prove to be a headache to United States authorities, attempting to curtail the insidious trade in captives.

By virtue of the Eleventh Article of the Treaty of Guadalupe Hidalgo, the United States was obligated to furnish some measure of security to Mexico by attempting to restrain Indian groups residing north of the international boundary. Included in that obligation was suppression of the trade in captives and plunder:

> It shall not be lawful, under any pretext whatever, for any inhabitant of the United States to purchase or acquire any Mexican, or any foreigner residing in Mexico, who may have been captured by Indians inhabiting the territory of either Republics, nor to purchase or acquire horses, mules, cattle, or property of any kind, stolen within Mexican territory by such Indians.[12]

This agreement did not end by establishing mere restrictions upon purchase of loot from marauding Indians. The treaty specified the release of individuals held in bondage:

> And in the event of any person or persons, captured within Mexican territory by Indians, being carried into the territory of the United States, the government of the latter engages and binds itself, in the most solemn manner, soon as it shall know of such captives being within its territory, and shall be able to do so through the faithful exercise of its influence and power to rescue them and return them to their country, or deliver them to the agent or representatives of the Mexican government.[13]

From the floor of Congress came a flood of claims that the United States possessed "both the ability and the will to restrain the Indians within the extended limits" of its territory. During the next few years Mexico was to question both the "will," as well as the "ability" of her northern neighbor to comply with its promises.

Officials of the United States knew nothing of the nature of its newly acquired territory; and even less of the Indians inhabiting the area. Perhaps the formulators of "Manifest Destiny" would have thought twice had they some inkling of costs involved in subduing marauding bands and living up to the promises of the Treaty of Guadalupe Hidalgo. Between 1849 and 1853 the United States attempted to put "teeth" into its treaty. As the Spanish government had done more than a hundred years before, Anglo-Americans began construction of a cordon of military posts. From the Gulf of Mexico to the confluence of the Colorado and Gila Rivers, one garrison after another was established. Between El Paso and Doña Ana, Fort Fillmore was built, as was Fort Conrad at Valverde; and Fort Webster followed soon after. Within a short span of three years four thousand rank and file were garrisoning a line from Texas to Fort Yuma.[14]

Despite the fact that many of the Anglo-American troops had come from battlefields of the Mexican War, they were nevertheless "green" in tactics applicable to frontier duty. Conditioning of cavalry mounts often rendered American units useless. Grain-fed and coddled animals were no match for Indian mustangs, which had undergone generations of adaptation to the arid and sparse environment of the southwest. The United States Army, however went to its task with a will —and its firepower and superior officership eventually decided the course of events within the area acquired through the Treaty of Guadalupe Hidalgo.

No defense line could be effective so long as Indian traders operated without government supervision—and it did not take long for officers and civil servants of the United States to realize that fact. James S. Calhoun had been Indian Agent but a few months when he wrote to the Commissioner of Indian Affairs that:

> The constant and unrestrained intercourse of traders with the Indians of this territory is, perhaps the greatest curse upon it, and so exceedingly pernicious is it, I have ventured to suggest to Governor Monroe, the propriety of extending by *Order,* the Laws of Congress in relation to trade . . . with Indian tribes . . .[15]

Calhoun not only enacted stringent regulations governing trade with tribes throughout New Mexico, he worked conscientiously to free Mexican captives in possession of marauding bands. Utilizing *Comancheros,* traders who knew Indian country and were accepted by otherwise hostile tribes, he succeeded in liberating a number of Mexicans. On June 27, 1850, thirteen Mexicans were turned over to José N. Prieto, at El Paso and within three months eight more were on their way to be reunited with their families in Mexico.[16]

Despite placement of garrisons on arteries of plunder, and the enactment of trade regulations, the Apaches and Comanches continued unrelenting in their attacks south of the border. Mexican states of Tamaulipes and San Luis Potosí were attacked by south Plains warriors; and Coahuila, Nueva León, and Chihuahua felt the brunt of both Apache and Comanche raids. Sonora—the worst hit of all north Mexican states—was pillaged solely by Apaches. The latter state suffered more due primarily to the lack of military posts restricting Apache incursions. Not until the mid-1850s would United States troops, in any number, be garrisoning points along its northern extremity.[17]

Unrelenting were Indian attacks upon Mexico—and chattel and loot continued to flow northward. From 1848 to 1853 United States troops tried in vain to stem depredations. With each raid that penetrated Mexico came a flood of complaints. Mexican ministers charged that Ango-Americans not only were powerless to stop the pillaging, but that garrisons offered an outlet for disposal of loot.[18] On October 5, 1853, James Gadsden, United States Minister to Mexico, forwarded a series of sharp-tongued letters to Army headquarters in Santa Fe, attempting to ferret out the truth of the matter:

There have been repeated complaints made to the mission of depredations committed by the savages, and claims preferred for indemnity under the 11th Article of the Treaty, that the garrison on or near the Mimbres [Fort Webster] . . . encourages, or permits an intercourse with the Indians, and they purchase from them Mexican prisoners, which the Indians bring in, or either permit, or do not prohibit American citizens from engaging in the traffic.[19]

It is doubtful that Anglo-American troops actually took a hand in the slave trade. Certainly during those early years the military was unable to exercise control over the trade. Traders knew the mountains, trails, and haunts of the Indians. These itinerant salesmen moved swiftly, and with relative impunity—and the army, in most cases, was powerless to stop them. Only time and political events would stem the trade in captives.

United States authorities, however, not only attempted to liberate captives already in possession of Indians, but in the hands of the middlemen as well. This was in part carried out by alerting various Indian agents to be on the lookout for Mexicans among tribesmen, returning from forays south of the international line. In October 1853 Governor of New Mexico and *ex officio* Superintendent of Indian Affairs, David Meriwether, issued a circulating letter to all agents under his jurisdiction:

> In regard . . . to the purchase or purchasing of Mexican captives held by our Indians, allow me to inform you that such a traffic can never be tolerated as this would be to offer a premium to the Indians to capture others.
>
> When you have it in your power to do so, you will reclaim and if necessary take by force any captives belonging to Mexico or the United States which may be found in the possession of the Indians of your agency, and forward to the Mexican consul near El Paso such as may belong to Mexico, taking his receipt for them, which you will forward to me, together with an account of the cost attending such reclamation and delivery.[20]

Slowly the army of the United States constricted the trade arteries over which chattel and loot flowed from Mexico into the Trans-Pecos southwest. Military posts and regular army patrols made it hazardous for Indians and traders to meet in large rendezvous; and creation of the reservation system made for easy surveillance. So too, did events in the arena of politics help slam the door closed in the face of the Indian slave trade. In

December of 1853 James Gadsden concluded negotiations for a vast land acquisition. At a cost of $10,000,000, the United States acquired from Mexico all the land in the southern part of New Mexico, south of the Gila, and from the Rio Grande westward to the Colorado River.[21]

Anglo troops were not long in occupying the area of the Gadsden Purchase; and a string of military posts were quickly erected. Fort Buchanan, on Sonoita Creek, was established in 1856; a garrison was maintained at Tucson; Camp Grant was built on the San Pedro in 1860; and Fort Bowie, in Apache Pass, followed in 1862. These military posts, together with a number of others, forged the final links in a chain of defense against Apaches—which eventually would bring total suppression.

With outbreak of the Civil War, Apaches sensed the reduction of United States forces; and again took to the warpath. Towns, ranchos, and mining districts throughout the southwest were attacked. This time, however, Apache marauding would be short-lived. Volunteer troops from California, New Mexico, and Colorado companies were not long in arriving upon the scene.

For the sake of defense, Arizona and New Mexico were divided and subdivided into military districts and sub-districts; and from posts within these jurisdictions regular patrols penetrated every canyon, ravine and mountain range. As the number of military posts and troops grew, so did the knowledge of Apachería, north of the international boundary.

Animosity which had long stood between various Apache bands, as well as with other tribes, was once again utilized—this time by Anglo-American commanders. Astute officers like General George Crook, Lieutenants Charles Gatewood, and Emmet Crawford, found as the Spanish had—that it was easier "to divide and conquer." Organization of Apache scouts under white officers quickly followed. No longer could hostile tribesmen find haven in the arid homeland—for on

47

their trail were men who knew the waterholes, trails, and encampments throughout Apacheria.

With military posts situated on every plunder trail leading in and out of Mexico; and Indian-led patrols scouting the country between—the day of Apache raiding was fast drawing to a close. Crashing defeats were dealt hostile tribesmen in 1872-73, turning the tide of battle in favor of the Anglo interlopers.[22] As the Spanish had done more than sixty years previous, the Apaches were again settled on reservations, and instructed in ways which were hoped would lead to self-sufficiency. Although the encroaching tide of Anglo settlers, and machinations of unscrupulous contractors and Indian Agents occasionally incited Apache bands to take to the warpath, the decade of the 1870s saw the gradual end of the Apache menace. Anglo-American firepower and influx of an almost overwhelming population had won out.

* * *

The halting of Indian forays south of the International Boundary closed forever the trade in chattel and loot. Rendezvous along the Rio Grande, Pecos, San Pedro, and Santa Cruz Rivers, and in adjacent sierras were either dominated by soldiers or being fenced by cattlemen. No longer were traders free to make pilgrimages to meet victorious war parties—harsh trade restrictions and military patrols had spelled the doom of these merchants.

Times had changed since the 1830s and 1840s, when Apaches rode virtually unmolested over all of northern Mexico. Then the basis of Indian raiding had been not only exaction of vengeance, which in many cases was justified, but was motivated by economics. The raiding pattern had become a well established tradition to Apaches, and their very existence now depended upon its maintenance. Mules, horses, bullion, and captives flowed northward into the hands of New Mexican and

Anglo-American traders; and from these men the Indians easily procured arms, powder, and shot. However, the surge of the Anglo-American frontier, with its military prowess, quickly alerted the scene.

From the 1870s on, those Apaches who took to the warpath did so for other motives—desperation sparked their depredations. The ruthless attempts to "brush aside the red men," either by complete removal or total annihilation; the machinations of Indian agents who manipulated their charges for personal gain, and narrow-minded military personnel, confused and often decimated the Apaches. Waning of tribal strength, confusion, and bewilderment inevitably leads to feelings of futility: then is the time where man—be he civilized or primitive—suicidally tries to extricate himself from the dilemma.

During the last agonizing years of Apache resistance, what captives were taken—and there were not many—did not pass into the hands of traders. Tribal strength was depleted, and Mexican, Anglo, and Piman children offered replacement for tribesmen fallen in battle. During the 1870s and 1880s Apache warriors did not hesitate to kill all "aliens" over the age of twelve. There was no sense keeping teenage boys, if they could not be disposed of to slave procurers. But younger children, and sometimes maidens, were usually brought home and adopted into the captor's family, or given to another Apache household that was less fortunate.

If they survived the ordeal of traveling with a rapidly moving war party and the initial impact of the harsh atmosphere of Apache camp-life, young tractable captives stood a fair chance of becoming the social equals of their captors. Captain John G. Bourke, chronicler of General George Crook, witnessed the termination of the 1886 Geronimo campaign, at which time he candidly observed a young captive—who, if retained by Apaches would in all likelihood have made the transition to Indian culture:

A group of little boys were romping freely and carelessly together; one of them seemed to be of Irish and Mexican lineage. After some persuasion he told Strauss and myself that his name was Santiago Mackin, captured at Mimbres, New Mexico; he seemed to be kindly treated by his young companions, and there was no interference with our talk, but he was disinclined to say much and was no doubt thoroughly scared. Beyond showing by the intelligent glance of his eyes that he fully comprehended all that was said to him in both Spanish and English, he took no further notice of us. He was about ten years old, slim, straight, and sinewy, blue-gray eyes, badly freckled, light eyebrows and lashes, much tanned and blistered by the sun, and wore an old and once white handkerchief on his head which covered it so tightly that the hair could not be seen. He was afterwards returned to his relatives in New Mexico.[23]

Although captives were viewed as chattel by Apaches, those that became "Indianized" often rose to be well-respected and beloved members of the tribe. During the latter phases of the Anglo-American occupation of the arid southwest, they were the intermediaries between white and red men, often assuming grave responsibilities for ironing out existing animosities. The stories behind many Indian captives would—and for that matter have—formed the plots for great works of fiction. The Mexican child torn from his family, and from his culture and society, by Apache marauders underwent a high degree of reorientation—and that process in itself is dramatic. But the agonizing, often unrelenting search—over periods of months and even years, by parents of captives adds that element of heartache and psychological impact so necessary for the writing of gripping literature.

* * *

1. For detailed study of problems confronting the United States in administering territory acquired by Treaty of Guadalupe Hidalgo see J. Fred Rippy, "The Indians of the Southwest in the Diplomacy of the United States and Mexico, 1848-1853," *Hispanic America Historical Review* (Vol. II, August 1919), pp. 363-396.

2. Ralph Smith, "Apache Plunder Trails Southward, 1831-1840," *New Mexico Historical Review* (Vol. XXXVIII, January 1962), pp. 20-42.

3. *Ibid.*; also Smith, "Mexican and Anglo-Saxon Trade in Scalps, Slaves, and Livestock, 1835-1841," *West Texas Historical Association Yearbook* (No. 36, 1960), pp. 98-115.

4. Annie H. Abel (comp. & ed.), *Official Correspondence of James S. Calhoun . . .* (Washington: 1915), p. 196. Hereafter cited as *Calhoun Correspondence.*

5. *Ibid.*, p. 162.

6. Calhoun to Brown, March 31, 1850; *Ibid.*, pp. 181-183.

7. Calhoun to Brown, March 31, 1850; in National Archives, Record Group 75, New Mexico Superintendency Papers.

8. Lieutenant Owen Chapman to Brevet Lieutenant Colonel Alexander, March 31, 1851; National Archives, Record Group 98, Department of New Mexico, Letters Received.

9. Captain D. Chandler to Major H. A. Nichols, August 10, 1854; in *ibid.*

10. Additional information on these communities can be found in the correspondence of: H. Randall to R. S. Robert, December 4, 1856; R. S. Robert to W. A. Nichols, November 29, 1856; D. Chandler to Nichols, August 10, 1854; J. W. Moore to J. D. Sturgis, February 26, 1855; in *ibid.*

11. Marcellus B. Edwards, *Marching with the Army of the West*, edited by Ralph P. Bieber (Glendale: Arthur H. Clark Co., 1936), p. 224.

12. Treaty of Guadalupe Hidalgo, copy in files of Arizona Pioneers' Historical Society, Tucson.

13. *Ibid.*

14. Rippy, *op. cit.*, pp. 383-384.

15. Calhoun to Commissioner of Indian Affairs, November 2, 1849; *Calhoun Correspondence*, p. 71.

16. *Ibid.*, pp. 227, 390-391, 406.

17. Rippy, *op. cit.*, p. 365.

18. Nichols to Richardson, December 15, 1853; Department of New Mexico.

19. *Ibid.*

20. Letter to David Meriwether (dated October 30, 1853), in Department of New Mexico.

21. For detailed study of Gadsden Purchase consult Louis B. Schmidt, "Manifest Opportunity and the Gadsden Purchase," *Arizona and the West* (Vol. III, Autumn 1961), pp. 245-264.

22. A devastating attack upon a large cave in Salt River Canyon in December 1872, resulted in the death of 75 Apaches. In early 1873 combined forces of infantry and cavalry assaulted the supposedly impregnable stronghold of Turret Butte. This attack defeated the hostile band residing there, and broke the backbone of resistance. See Arthur Woodward (ed.), *On the Bloody Trail of Geronimo* (Los Angeles: Westernlore Press, 1958), p. xiv.

23. John G. Bourke, *On the Border with Crook* (New York: Charles Scribner's Sons, 1892), p. 477.

III

Despite popular belief, the Apache menace did not end with surrender of hostile bands in the 1870s and 1880s—it continued instead for the next fifty years. As late as the 1920s Apaches were still at large in the rugged mountains of southern Arizona, New Mexico, and the Mexican states of Sonora and Chihuahua—and these Indians plundered and murdered as did their cousins who rode with Victorio, or Geronimo years before. Indeed, so serious did their depredations become, that by 1926 Mexican authorities deemed it expedient to suppress these marauders. The call went forth for Indian fighters; Mexican cavalry units were alerted; volunteers flocked to the border towns of Naco, Douglas, and Nogales to join in what would be the west's last Indian campaign.

Like all previous Indian trackdowns, a single incident touched off this massive manhunt—which would make headlines and capture, for years to come, the front pages of newspapers, both in Mexico and the United States. One man was responsible for this dramatic story, which reads like fiction. Francisco Fimbres —a rancher from the Bavispe Valley of northern Sonora—launched this hunt with a spirit of vengeance nursed for years against Apaches. They had murdered his wife before his very eyes, and had kidnapped his year-old son.

Ranches and small agricultural settlements stretching for nearly 200 miles southward from the International Boundary were plagued repeatedly by Apaches, who swept down from their lairs in the Sierra Madres to drive off livestock and harass travelers. During one such incursion in 1913 these Indians struck at the Fimbres rancho, slaughtering cattle for subsistence and driving off a number of horses. Alert vaqueros discovered the mischief and pursuit was organized within hours. Francisco Fimbres and his hard-riding ranchhands caught the Apaches as they crossed the range for safety of the mountains to the east. In the running battle that ensued, several Indians were killed and a fourteen-year-old squaw captured.[1]

Following tradition which had been established more than two hundred years before, Fimbres kept this Apache girl as recompense for the destruction wreaked by her clansmen. Lupe—as she was dubbed—was a tractable person; and in the years to come she developed into a trusted house servant and nurse for the Fimbres children. The Apaches, however, never forgot Lupe. Enraged, they struck back. Cattle were driven from the Fimbres rancho in large numbers; and so often did their attacks come that vaqueros feared for their lives. For more than thirteen years these conditions persisted—until 1926, at which time the Apaches exacted their final vengeance.

It was a crisp morning in mid-October of that year when Francisco, his wife, daughter and Heraldo, his infant son, set out on horseback from Naco to return to their ranch. For several hours the party leisurely rode and discussed bits of gossip picked up at the border town. As the ranchero and his family neared the foothills of the Sierra Madre Mountains and the town of Nacori Chico, a volley of shots blasted from a dense mesquite thicket close beside the trail.[2] Señora Fimbres, riding a short distance ahead of her husband and carrying his son, went down—wounded. Francisco, grabbing the reins of his daughter's mount, quickly made for the cover of a nearby arroyo. While Francisco dismounted, grabbed his rifle, and pushed his daughter to the safety of the river bank, the Indians had rushed to the stricken woman, grabbed the infant—and sensing life still within the woman, cut her throat with a quick stroke.[3]

By the time Francisco reached his wife, there was little he could do. And the Apaches had faded away as swiftly as they had appeared.

Tormented by sight of the slaughter of his wife and abduction of his son, Francisco Fimbres planned immediate pursuit to free his son and avenge his wife's death. As he was not the only rancher in northern Sonora to be harassed by these savages, he sought governmental aid for his quest—for he could never finance an adequate expedition into the rugged Sierra Madre Mountains. Francisco, however, ran into immediate opposition from Sonoran officials—owing to the fact that the Apaches were believed to be encamped in the same general area where General Obregon had waged his successful campaign against the Yaquis; and it was feared that any movements of large numbers of troops would once again incite the now peaceful, yet still very militant tribe.

Refused aid from Sonora authorities, Francisco utilized every means at his disposal to organize a reprisal expedition. He interrogated Lupe, the Apache girl. But she cautioned against pursuit of her people by large numbers of men. For that would invariably bring death to his son—if it had not already occurred. Furthermore, the band resided in one of the most inaccessible areas of the Sierra Madres, impossible for a large expedition with cumbersome supply trains to reach.

Francisco Fimbres would do his best to carry the search forward on his own—using only his vaqueros, who were familiar with the serrated ridges that make up that great, rugged cordillera dividing Sonora from Chihuahua.

The years slowly passed, and the ranchero and his vaqueros carried their search into the mountains whenever feasible—but without success, for the Apaches camped on the high ridges and remained ever vigilant against surprise. Trails grew dim. The dense growths of scrub oak, and the eroded, deeply gashed mountains repeatedly turned Fimbres back. Numerous failures, however, failed to daunt him—for he still nursed his vengeance. He would not give up, for abandoned campsites often showed indications of children—one of which could be his.

Hope that he might still free Heraldo burned within Francisco; and he again sought the aid of Sonoran officials. By January 1929 tension with the Yaquis had eased and revolutionary fervor had been quelled, at least momentarily. Permission was at last granted allowing Fimbres to organize a full scale undertaking. With authority from Governor Fausto Topete, the expedition would be assembled at Agua Prieta, just across the international boundary from the Arizona town of Douglas. The expedition would not be large in terms of manpower and equipment. It would, instead, be a heavily armed and highly maneuverable group. Eleven men would form an advance party to flush the Indians out of hiding. Fifty more would wait the word at Agua Prieta to close upon the Apaches.

On January 5 the advance group, led personally by Fimbres, was ready to move out. They went by truck as far as the Mormon settlement of Colonia Morales, thence eastward, where they entered on horseback the wild canyons of the Sierra Madres,[4] by way of a gap near Rusbayo, known as Batepito.

All northern Mexico and the Anglo-American states of Arizona and New Mexico waited, as the expedition threaded its way over one massive escarpment after another. Up through the dense oak thickets which grew at lower elevations and into the pine forests above 6000 feet, Fimbres led his riders. And back at Agua Prieta picked men stood ready to augment the punitive force, should a runner bring word that reinforcements were needed. Of these volunteers many were veteran Indian fighters. Sam Hayhurst, expert trailer who had tracked the very same Apache band when it raided the Diamond A Ranch in 1922, was there; and Anton Massonovich, ex-cavalryman and veteran of the Geronimo campaign had tendered his services.[5]

The days dragged by. No word from Fimbres came, and fears were aroused that perhaps he and his men had been ambushed by the Indians. This anxiety, however, was lifted by appearance of Ramon Quejada on the night of January 11. This member of the advance group was brought into Agua Prieta by a Chinese vegetable grower. Racked with fever, and in an almost delirious state, Quejada related that he had left the expedition before it reached the Canyon of the Caves— where the group had left their horses and proceeded on foot. Until that time, no Indian signs had been encountered; and Fimbres' progress had been hampered by snowfalls and freezing temperatures.

Quejada's report made the Presidente of Agua Prieta, Rogerio Loreta, apprehensive for the safety of the group; and Jesus Valdez, an expert trailer, was ordered to "start immediately and back track Quejada into the Sierras," and report back to Agua Prieta on January 14. So urgent was the desire to establish communications with Fimbres, that Valdez' orders bore the implicit instruction to "commandeer transportation for coming out and to ask aid if needed."[6]

Valdez left that night; and traveling first by truck and then by horseback, overtook Fimbres a day later, some forty miles east of Rusbayo. The tracker reported "that the Fimbres party, which had increased from twelve to fifteen men, had sent for additional supplies.

57

Although it had encountered severe hardships in the mountains, due to the extreme cold, the party nevertheless was determined to carry on."

On the night of January 31, however, Fimbres and his tired followers returned to civilization—without Apache scalps or his son, but not without information and hope. They had, after reaching the Canyon of the Caves, encountered signs that the Apache band numbered about a dozen bucks, several women, and possibly three children about the size of Heraldo. Although the Indians had been flushed from their camp, Fimbres believed that they would seek sanctuary again in the remote area about the Canyon of the Caves.[7] And Francisco vowed to renew the search.

Within a week of his return from the Sierras, Francisco had laid plans for a new expedition before the governor of Hermosillo. This second venture promised to be the largest since the Geronimo campaign of 1886. Aided by Ricardo Topete, brother of the Sonoran governor, and Rogerio Loreto, President of Agua Prieta, the expedition would be sufficiently equipped to withstand the privations of the isolated Apache country. By end of November 1929 the plans had been carefully worked out. Both civilian and military contingents would launch a pincer movement against the Indians—this time the Apaches would not escape.

In charge of recruiting the civilian portion of the expedition, Francisco Fimbres chose his men carefully, for only the hardiest could endure the rigors of this campaign. Newspapers played up the story. Headlines flashed across the United States—"this trackdown would be the West's last Indian roundup." Into the office of Leslie Gatliff, Chief of Police at Douglas—who was acting as recruiting officer for Fimbres—came offers of assistance from adventurers, thrill-seekers, and soldiers of fortune. Fifteen hundred applicants from eighteen American states, most Canadian provinces, as well as many Mexican states, volunteered for service in the hazardous enterprise.

"Have you room," inquired Ellsworth G. Drazy of Dwight, Illinois, "for a fellow who has done two hitches in the Marine Corps and one in the Navy? I never fought Indians, but I have chased Spicks all around Haiti and Nicaragua and was in the landing and occupation at Vera Cruz. I guess I'll have the guts to chase these birds."

From Denver, Colorado, Dr. R. G. Davenport wrote: "If you contemplate going after those Indians soon I shall count it a great privilege to join you. I have hunted big game in many parts of America, but I am sure shooting an Apache Indian would give me a greater thrill than any I have heretofore shot at."

"I have traveled all over the globe," claimed Jack Williams, of Kenora, Ontario, Canada, "seen a bit of life, fought men of all colors, so I would like to become one of your expedition, for I love action."

Whatever the individual reasons for joining the Fimbres expedition might be—there was one underlying motive for all applicants: The spirit behind the many enlistments was voiced in a letter from Irving Swanson, of Clarkdale, Arizona, who with a friend had tendered their services: "This will probably be the only opportunity offered us having any degree of military experience and adventure. Won't you please let us join your band?"[8]

Thus the letters poured in, but only a fraction of the many applicants could be chosen. In the meantime, the Mexican Federal Army made preparations to uphold its end of the expedition against the Indians. Colonel Hermenegildo Carrillo, with two hundred cavalrymen from the Sonora barracks, established a base of operations at Bacerac, at the foot of the Sierra Madres. From that point contact would be maintained both by telephone and automobile with civilian contingents, headquartered at Douglas and Agua Prieta.[9] Enormous as the plans for this Apache roundup were threatening to become, the campaign was destined never to be launched.

In the northern provinces of Mexico people were restless over political injustice and usurpation by wealthy landowners—and revolution was imminent in the first months of 1930. So too, were Mexican authorities becoming more and more suspicious of the numbers of Anglo thrill-seekers who would invade her soil in quest of Apache hair. In the past, the northern provinces had witnessed repeated attempts by Americans, north of the international boundary, to wrest control and to aid revolutionary spirit. This Apache campaign could indeed furnish another pretext for reckless Anglo-American movements. The Mexican consul at Agua Prieta closed the border to all volunteer Indian fighters, and the nearest federal garrison was mobilized to back up the government's actions—by force if necessary.[10]

Heartbreaking as this collapse of the proposed expedition may have been to Francisco Fimbres, it did not deter him from carrying on the search for his lost son. Apache incursions against the ranches of the Bavispe Valley had not diminished in either number or intensity —and if the government would do nothing to protect its citizens, they must continue to deal with the Indians in their own way. So, as they had usually done in the past, the ranchers organized, pooling their own resources of men and equipment. They were resolved to make this the final annihilation of the menace.

During early March 1930 the "profitable" encounter with the marauders occurred. Five ranchers from the Bacerac district intercepted the Apache band as it was running off horses and cattle. In the fight that followed, five Indians paid with their lives. The remainder of the band, however, escaped; and for the next couple of years Sonoran ranchers methodically tracked them. Francisco took three scalps himself, and his brother, Cayatano, several more. But Heraldo—the Fimbres child—was never located. As hope for the recovery of his son faded, Francisco's personal vendetta grew against the Apaches. And he patiently waited for a chance to deliver the death blow.

Late in November of 1935, when snows in the high mountains forced the Indians to subsistence found on lower ranges, the trap was sprung. Francisco, Cayatano, and a group of vaqueros had carefully staked out a small herd of cattle in an arroyo near the Fimbres ranch. With a carefully baited trap, Francisco Fimbres lured the Apaches to almost the very spot where the drama opened so many years before. Two young male warriors and the several females were quickly dispatched. With the sound of the first rifle shot, the Indians scattered—the survivors fleeing for the safety of higher elevations. However, the Fimbres men were in close pursuit, and they too knew the country. Backtracking the trail, Cayatano and Francisco followed the Indians to the upper reaches of Canyon de Nutria, northwest of Tres Rios—and there finished the job.

Carefully the bodies of the slain Apaches were searched for some evidence which might reveal a clue as to Heraldo's fate. Nothing was found. After nearly ten years Francisco Fimbres had taken his revenge. But he had not recovered his son; and the worry and strain of the many pursuits had aged him beyond his years. Although presumed dead, the fate of Heraldo Fimbres, will never be determined. Like the mystery shrouding the disappearance of so many other children presumed to have been kidnaped by Apaches, the abduction of Heraldo already is being embellished by the "folk process." Across many tables, before many camp fires, and in many *cantinas,* the slaughter of Senora Fimbres, the captivity of Heraldo, and the frenzied search by a man bent upon vengeance, is to this day being recounted.

1. Douglas, *Silver Belt,* January 5, 1929; Tucson *Daily Star,* January 10, 1929.
2. Tucson *Citizen,* February 1, 1929.
3. *Ibid.,* January 5, 1929.
4. *Ibid.*; also *Daily Silver Belt,* January 5, 1929.

5. *Citizen*, January 7, 1929.
6. *Star*, January 12, 1929, January 15, 1929.
7. *Citizen*, February 1, 1929.
8. *Star*, January 31, 1930.
9. *Citizen*, November 30, 1929.
10. Bisbee *Daily Review*, April 6, 1930.

Slave Raiding and the Navajo Wars 1700-1885

I

The Navajo people have suffered considerably at the hands of historians—who contend that this tribe has been the cause of two centuries of warfare. When the documentary record is consulted, and analyzed in terms of present-day ethnological data, a far different picture emerges—and it is a picture not at all favorable to the white man. It is true Athapascan peoples (Apaches and Navajos of today) were intimately involved in hostilities with the Spanish from the period before the Pueblo Rebellion (1680), until the 1880s. The Navajos, however, did not make war just to steal and kill; they earned their reputation as warriors fighting to protect their lands, property, and families—and a just cause it was. But the tribe paid a price: for in various engagements between 1690 until the return of Navajos from Bosque Redondo in 1868, nearly one thousand tribesmen died in battle—and if documentation could be complete, this figure would undoubtedly be much higher. But what is even more shocking is that church records reveal more than 1600 Navajos were baptized in churches throughout New Mexico, for the similar period. These individuals were not converts. They were women and children, carried into captivity by New Mexico slaving expeditions, and placed as menials in homes of the landed gentry. In view of these facts, a reappraisal must be made of Navajo tribal history for the period from 1700 until 1870.[1]

The Spaniards entered the arid Southwest with one desire—to conquer native peoples in the name of "Glory, God, and Gold." By the early 1600s the Pueblos of the Rio Grande Valley had been "reduced," and were firmly under Spanish control. The less sedentary groups, like the Athapascans, Utes, and Comanches, however, were better able to resist Spanish efforts. These people fought against direct assault, subtle missionary activity—and that eventual standard policy of Spain—of playing one tribe against another.

By 1680 the Pueblos had had enough of white men's ways, and with support of Athapascan groups staged a successful revolt. Together, they drove the Spaniards down the Rio Grande Valley to where present-day El Paso is located. For twelve years the Indians of the Southwest had freedom. But as soon as that spark which united them died away, the Spaniards returned —and Indian resistance crumbled in the face of well equipped troops.

During this conflict, as in the case of any war, peoples were displaced. Pueblo peoples who did not wish to submit to the yoke of Spanish authority sought sanctuary among more isolated tribes to the west and north. Fleeing Hispanic vengeance many Puebloans settled with the Athapascans residing in north-central New Mexico, and in the area of Cañons Blanco and Largo. There in *Dinetah* (Old Navajo Country) as it is known, they continued to resist with help from the protectors. Although return of the Spanish was in such force that they could not be beaten back, the combination of Athapascan and Puebloan were successful in other ways. Together they gradually developed a new life-way—which is characterized today by the name—Navajo.

As conflict with the Spanish gradually subsided, economic prosperity reigned for nearly fifty years. By the late 1740s missionaries were seeking converts among the Navajo; and Franciscan missions were founded especially for that tribe at Cebolleta and Encinal. Priests soon realized that Navajo ethics and religious values were incompatible with Christian ideology; and that the "heathens only assembled so long as annuities were forthcoming." By end of the 1750s the Navajo mission program had collapsed. Although it was very apparent that this tribe could not be successfully "reduced," active military operations did not immediately commence.

A far more insidious element was at work, gnawing at the shaky foundation of Spanish-Navajo relations. By mid 1750, as historian Frank Reeve points out, "the basic relation between the two people shifted from a religious to a territorial problem. Spanish settlers slowly penetrated the valley of the Rio Puerco of the East and the Cebolleta area . . ."[2] slowly and menacingly the tide of encroachment flowed from the Rio Abajo. Spanish ranches were established between the Rio Puerco and Cebolleto Mountains, and around the northwest and southwest base of the red cap of that range, Mt. Taylor.[3] At first the tribe welcomed the intruders, for they promised protection from Utes to the north, who frequently raided across the Rio San Juan.

Conflict soon became apparent as settlers infiltrated the eastern margin of Navajoland, carrying with them land grants—which the Indians little understood. So too, did Spanish flocks and herds tempt Navajo *pobres,* who sought to increase their status among fellow tribesmen. Added to these factors was the Spanish courting of the Utes, the latter tribe offering strong economic and diplomatic advantages. Late in 1773 Governor Mendinueta, of New Mexico, secretly agreed to remain neutral in a war which Utes proposed to wage against the Navajo. In so doing, the governor hoped to push back the Navajo frontier, thus making more land available to Spanish settlement.[4]

Crossing the Rio San Juan, Ute raiding parties swarmed down upon Navajo *rancherias,* killing many tribesmen, destroying planting grounds, and carrying women and children into captivity—the latter whom they disposed of to Spanish middlemen at the annual trade fair held at Taos. The pressure from Ute attacks, sanctioned by the Spanish, profoundly affected Navajo population movement—and this effect is not clearly understood to this day. At any rate, in the face of repeated Ute onslaughts, a gradual exodus from the *Dinetah* country occurred. Navajos began to drift westward toward Cañon de Chelly and southwest into the Cebolleta and Chuska Mountains.[5]

The Diné were not long in discovering the source of Ute attacks—and they struck at Rio Grande and Rio Puerco settlements with vengeance, driving out many Spanish settlers who had usurped tribal lands. The Spanish defended the line of settlement as best they could. During spring of 1774 Governor Mendinueta sent against the Navajo two expeditions composed primarily of Pueblo auxiliaries. Back to Laguna, Acoma and into the environs of Albuquerque were carried forty-six Navajo women and children. Consultation of baptismal records quickly reveal the fate of these captives—as indicated by one entry, translated by ethnohistorians David Brugge and J. Lee Correll:

In this Mission of Señor San Joseph de la Laguna on the third day of . . . June 1778, I, Fray Tomas Salvador Fernandez, Minister and Teacher of the Doctrine of this mission, baptized solemnly . . ., and blessed as is directed by the Roman ritual a child of three years of age, to whom I gave the name Rosalia, Indian of the Navajo Nation, servant in this pueblo to Polina Trasiztcha, who she has recognized as mother from the age of three.[6]

From this baptism of a Navajo captured three years previous—and at the height of conflict—can be gleaned a partial explanation for subsequent Navajo suspicion. Although the Spanish successfully subdued the Diné for the moment, the seeds of fear had been firmly implanted in the minds of the tribe. Before 1773 Navajos welcomed Spanish missionaries. Hispanic treachery, in the form of secret alliances with their mortal enemies, seriously shook Navajo trust. Even after termination of the war, the tribe suffered from Spanish machinations. During the next eight years—so called peaceful years as historians relate—thirteen Navajo children were baptized at Acoma and Laguna. All these individuals are recorded as being either "servants" or as being "purchased."[7] In all probability this figure would be much higher, if other church records had been consulted. Regardless, these thirteen captives offer evidence that expeditions were going against the Navajos; and it is these slaving parties (which in all likelihood were composed of Utes and Puebloans) that hastened Navajo population drift toward the Chuska-Tunicha Mountains and beyond, into the Cañon de Chelly or Chinle drainage area.[8] In the face of an omnipresent danger— the encroachment upon tribal land and slave raiding— it would be only a matter of time before warfare would erupt between the Navajo and Spanish.

Mt. Taylor, or "Turquoise Mountain" as Navajos call it, situated between present-day Gallup and Albuquerque, New Mexico, has always been part of traditional Navajoland; and figures prominently in tribal mythology. Not only does its barren reddish peak mark the southern boundary of *Dinetah,* but allegedly it is the abode of many Navajo dieties, around which a number of tribal ceremonials revolve. Cebolleta, on the southeast slope of Mt. Taylor, had become a thorn in the side of Navajo. Founded first as a mission, which failed, this town now served as the jumping-off point for all Spanish encroachments and military reconnaissances against the tribe.

When demands by Navajo headmen that this settlement be evacuated were refused by New Mexican officials, hostilities were renewed. Raids followed against Spanish herders and livestock grazing along the Rio Puerco of the East; but the real blow came during the summer of 1804, when nearly 1,000 Navajo warriors laid siege to Cebolleta itself. So hard-pressed were the town's defenders that the governor lamented that "everything must be done to keep the site of Cebolleta occupied." To secure their foothold on the edge of Navajoland, New Mexican militia launched a campaign in August, resulting in fifty-seven Navajo warriors being killed and five women and children taken captive. But this did not quell the wrath of the Navajo, and desperately the governor requested and received aid from Sonora. Lieutenant Antonio Narbona marched from Arizpe with a relief column, composed of Spanish troops and Opata Indian auxiliaries. With fresh support New Mexican officialdom immediately launched a winter campaign against the Diné. The victory note was sounded on January 17, 1805, when Sonoran, Opata, and New Mexican forces marched upon Cañon de Chelly. In that surprise attack, 115 aged males and females were annihilated; and thirty-three young women and children captured.

Long speculated by historians as taking place at the famous Massacre Cave, in upper Cañon del Muerto, this attack broke the backbone of Navajo resistance. Following Spanish policy, the captives were considered booty, and distributed among worthy troops—eleven Navajos being given to militiamen from New Mexico, and the remaining twenty-three were presented to Sonoran soldiers and their Opata companions.[9]

The fate of these Navajo women and children is predictable. A search through records of the Parish of Arizpe reveals nearly a dozen "Apache" baptismals during early spring of 1805. This would have allowed more than enough time for return of Narbona's column, and for his booty to be processed according to

Spanish tradition—which is the conversion by baptism of all "heathen" captives. As church records give no precise designation as to tribal affiliation (*e.g.* Coyotero, Lipan, Gila, or Navajo), it is indeed likely that these children were among the captives distributed to Narbona's troops. As was customary, these "Apache" captives received the "blessed waters and oils" and assumed the names of their godparent—in this case, the soldier or Opata auxiliary into whose care they were placed.[10]

*   *   *

To the east of New Mexican settlement—upon the Great Plains—the situation with Indian tribes was deepening and would eventually directly affect the Navajos. As a result of European power struggles during the early 18th century, tribes such as Pawnee, Comanche, Kiowa, and Plains Apache were receiving large quantities of weapons, powder, and shot. From posts along the Missouri, Platte, Arkansas Rivers, and throughout Texas, French traders were keeping close watch upon Spanish movements, and at the same time dispersing large amounts of contraband in exchange for mules pilfered from Mexico.[11]

The introduction of French arms greatly altered the economic and diplomatic picture between the Spanish and the Indian. Slave raiders who had previously preyed upon these tribes now had good reason to be apprehensive—for a Comanche armed with a flintlock was a formidable adversary. As was standard procedure in Spanish-Indian policy, when a tribe became a power threat—as in the case of south Plains peoples— it was often easier to court it as an ally. So it was that Spanish officials in New Mexico deemed it expedient to gain the alliance of rapidly arming Plains tribes. This was accomplished in the late 1700s by Juan Bautista de Anza—and from that time forward the Spanish, Mestizo, and Pueblo Indian population in New Mexico was tied economically to Plains Indians. The day of the *Comanchero*—that itinerant trader who ventured far out into the central plains to peddle his wares—had begun.[12]

With establishment of a symbiotic relationship between the Spanish and Plains peoples, the trade fair became commonplace in New Mexican communities adjacent to the central grasslands. And to these annual events came a multitude of Plains Indians to offer their goods—and chattel. As Taos, on the upper Rio Grande, afforded easy access, it soon became the rendezvous point. As Friar Dominguez comments, it must have been truly a lively spot:

> When the [Comanches] are on their good behavior, or at peace, they enter Taos to trade. At this fair they sell buffalo hides, horses, mules, buffalo meat, pagan Indians (of both sexes, children and adults) whom they capture from other nations . . . They also sell good guns, pistols, powder, balls, tobacco, hatchets, and some vessels of yellow tin . . . They are great traders, for as soon as they buy anything, they usually sell exactly what they bought; and usually they keep losing, the occasion when they gain being very rare, because our people ordinarily play infamous tricks on them. In short, the trading day resembles a second-hand market in Mexico, the way people mill about.[13]

Secure in their alliance with the Spanish, and armed with French trade weapons, the Comanches turned their aggression northward and to the west toward the Utes, Pawnees, Apaches, and Navajos. Plains raiders frequently crossed the entire length of New Mexico to attack the Diné, Intermountain and Basin tribes. The Navajos correctly assumed that the Spanish were behind these attacks, and the excessive protestations and denials by New Mexican officials suggest the plaguing

72

of guilty conscience. Suspicions reached the breaking point in 1818; and encroachment upon Navajo land led to open hostility. This war, however, was short-lived, and a treaty was concluded a year later.

During this interim of peace an attempt was made to iron out the long-standing land controversy. The obvious solution to the problem—as far as the Spanish were concerned—was complete removal of the Navajos. The governor proposed that the tribe be driven across the Colorado River into California. However, troops in adequate numbers to carry out this feat were not available; and New Mexico had to rely upon treaty stipulations as an alternative. Complete Navajo removal would have to wait for nearly fifty years.

An ill-defined boundary line between tribal domain and Spanish settlements was drawn up and confirmed, and the right was upheld for New Mexican stockmen to graze beyond the line, as far as Cañon Largo. As might be expected, ambitions for land again led to an explosive situation. By spring of 1822 Governor Facundo Melgares was cautioning outlying settlements that the Navajos "may attempt a bloody vengeance upon inhabitants of the province"; and the general populace was warned to prepare for attacks.[14] A general levy of men and equipment soon followed. So too, were plans forthcoming for a concerted movement of troops from Chihuahua and Sonora.[15]

These elaborate military precautions momentarily intimidated the Navajos, and treaty negotiations were once again opened. It is rather revealing that land issues and boundaries were now of little importance—for nearly every treaty clause bore directly upon the subject of Indian captivity, as illustrated by terms of the proposed treaty between Navajos and the Province of New Mexico, drawn up on February 5, 1823:

1. That all captives which the Navajos may have made of our people be returned without hid-

ing any, and the same with the fugitives, if there are any.

2.   That there be returned to them those who fled to us; whenever they may wish to go back; but if they should wish to receive the saving waters of Baptism, it does not appear the desire of Catholics to deny them, before favoring them on the contrary, and exhorting them to the end that the number of faithful adoring the True God of the Christians is multiplied.

3.   That it be demanded of them to the last that they return what they have stolen in the Province, from the last peace celebrated; returning to the injured what was robbed, in its entirety.

4.   And lastly, that it be energetically proposed to them that they be converted to the Cath-reducing themselves to Pueblos . . .[16]

It is pathetic, however, that at the very time of peace conference the governor and his lieutenants were debating how to divide the booty and captives which the forthcoming campaign would surely net.[17] Without waiting to see if tribesmen would comply with their new treaty, a plan of war was drafted by New Mexican leaders. A campaign of 1,000 men would be launched.

As New Mexican officials well knew—the Navajos did not, and could not, live up to treaty stipulations; and the newly-appointed governor, José Antonio Vizcarra, launched the campaign during spring. For four months Navajoland was scoured by troops, a detachment penetrating to the "Elephant Feet," west of present-day Kayenta, Arizona. For such a massive operation, this campaign was a failure as far as ferreting out the illusive Indian. Only fifty warriors were killed, and thirty-six women and children taken captive, to be divided among the command—"as booty."[18]

By January 1824 Governor Vizcarra was at last optimistic that he had "created harmony in this unhappy Province."[19] His optimism, however, was totally unfounded, for his campaign had served only to increase Navajo hatred. The Diné was becoming aware of one fact: that they were surrounded by enemies. The Utes to the north, Puebloans to the east, and even their cousins, the Apaches to the south, were being used against them—and these people were being paid, not in trade goods or currency, but by being awarded Navajo women and children to be disposed of as they saw fit.

Navajo hatred was well-founded. As the treaty of 1823, as well as subsequent ones hint at, this was a time when the tribe became a major source of captives for the slave trade. The decade of the 1820s witnessed numerous sanctioned and clandestine slaving expeditions against the Navajo; and there are over 250 recorded baptismals of Navajo captives for this period. If entries in ecclesiastical documents identified those captives listed only as "Indians," this total would undoubtedly be doubled.[20]

* * *

Mexico's fight for independence directly influenced conditions in New Mexico. Throughout that country's far north—in Chihuahua, Sonora, and New Mexico—frontier defenses crumbled as morale hit its lowest ebb. Garrisons were plagued by desertions, disobedience, and open revolt. And more than ever the slave raiders operated freely—often with governmental sanction, for these were the only means at hand for intimidating the Indians.

With the collapse of centralized government throughout Mexico, newly formulated treaties with Indian tribes never saw ratification—and such was the case with Vizcarra's treaty.[21] Tribes throughout northern Mexico were quick to comprehend the far-reaching effect of this breakdown of military protection and morale—and the Navajos were no exception. By 1827 reports of Navajo depredations were daily occurrence. Throughout that summer, and into 1828, this tribe struck. For the next few years their vicious attacks were leveled at slave-raiding centers, such as Abiquiu, Cebolleta, Jemez, and Cubero. By 1832 tribal warriors were becoming unusually bold in their forays. Twice during the first week of October, Navajos raided the military detachment at Socorro and the Comandante General Inspector lamented that "the troops were unable to give chase, because they have no horses."[22]

Organization of Mexican reprisal expeditions were the natural aftermath of Navajo raiding. During the summer of 1834 the governor sanctioned a number of slave raiding campaigns. The Pueblos of Sandia, Jemez and Cochiti contributed men, as did Cebolleta, Cubero, and Abiquiu. As usual, these reprisal expeditions served only to invoke Navajo wrath.

For three years the war seesawed back and forth, with Navajos raiding New Mexican ranchos and settlements, and the New Mexicans retaliating. In December of 1837 a campaign was launched against the tribe. Rancherias near Ojo del Gallo, Chuska, and Cañon de Chelly were laid waste—twenty Indians were surprised and killed, nearly twenty more taken as slaves, and 7,000 sheep captured.[23]

In the fall of 1838, Governor Manuel Armijo marched against the tribe, and delivered an even more demoralizing blow. This time seventy-eight warriors were killed, seventy-six of both sexes captured, and 2,000 sheep and 1,200 sacks of corn taken from the Navajos. The devastation to crops, and the wails of squaws for their children, carried into slavery, convinced Navajo leaders that it would be wise to sue for peace.

On July 15, 1839, another treaty was enacted at Jemez. Following this agreement, Navajo leaders frequently requested return of their people held in bondage—and they even offered to exchange Mexicans held by the tribe. Governor Manuel Armijo, however, tenaciously protected the slave trader and the wealthy gentry owning Indian captives. He sternly refused to even discuss the matter with Indian leaders, "because the conduct of Navajos since the treaty had not been good."[24]

Armijo's words proved true, for the Diné would never hold to any agreement so long as their children were servants of New Mexicans. With coming of fall the entire line of settlement, from Socorro to Abiquiu was pillaged by Navajo war-parties. For the next year Governor Armijo launched punitive expeditions, finally humbling the Diné enough to extract, on March 10, 1841, another shaky peace.

This worthless treaty, concluded at Santo Domingo, was designed "to alleviate any resentment Navajo chieftains had against the Mexicans"; by forbidding the taking of "slaves and captives by both sides." It further specified that the "entire Navajo tribe, in all parts of the Republic, is obliged to turn over all captives"; and that "any captives of the Navajos who are among Mexican citizens and who succeed in escaping their masters, the Government will not take action to reclaim them."[26]

On the day of the treaty consummation, tribal headmen returned four Mexican captives—but not willingly. Indian resentment ran deeper than just ink upon paper. Mexican military expeditions and slave raiders had destroyed crops, burned hogans, stolen sheep, and claimed as slaves, Navajo children. Anger of the headmen was apparent when they bitterly complained "that ten times they had returned captives—and at no time had the Mexicans returned theirs."[27]

It came as no surprise to Mexican officials when Navajo raiding commenced. The slave raiders, aided by New Mexican officialdom, could once again deal a profitable hand in Indian affairs. Small parties of men, numbering no more than fifty or sixty—for larger groups only slowed travel—were assembled at towns in close proximity to Navajoland. Included were Puebloans, Utes, and other Indians carrying grudges against the Diné, and these predatory bands moved rapidly and silently through Navajo country. Swooping down on rancherías, putting to death those tribesmen who either had no commercial value, or who resisted, they carried away women and children, as well as livestock, blankets, and anything else of value.

When a slaving expedition returned to its base of operation, it might outwardly appear as though it had not been at all successful. Perhaps six to twelve women and children would be tied to saddlehorns; and a caravan of mules, burdened with blankets and trinkets might follow, together with any livestock taken in the course of their raids.

By mid 1820s, however, a gradual change had come to the economic system of Mexico's frontier. A flow of hard currency was at last making its way northward, and the barter system was giving way to much sounder bargaining—at least so far as the middle men in the slave trade were concerned. No longer were the final transactions for captives carried out in terms of livestock, blankets, hides, and weapons. Navajo children now brought 75 to 150 pesos apiece. And this amount, added to the receipts for sheep and other booty, was indeed a sizeable sum. The profits of subsistence agriculture and herding, as practiced at that time in New Mexico, never equalled what was realized by serving three months with a slaving enterprise.

* * *

The effects of slave raiding upon the Navajos will never be fully comprehended—but what fragmentary data is available points to far reaching consequences. It has been postulated that Ute raiding—and their raids were conducted primarily as slaving raids—together with Spanish treachery, was a factor behind the Navajo's movement west and southwest. By 1800 Navajo bands had well established the present location of the tribe. Tribesmen were residing in the sinuous rincons of the Chuska-Tunicha Mountains; and in the deep gorges of the Chinle drainage basin. So too, were they beginning to push west over Black Mesa toward the Hopi villages. Whether the movement of Navajos toward Hopi was spurred by slave raiding is anyone's guess. However, Black Mesa was a primary target of slaving expeditions at the advent of the Anglo-American period (1846). With active pursuit of slave raiding during the 1820s certain Navajo bands had begun to align themselves with still other peoples. The San Juan Paiutes—also target of Ute and Mexican forays—felt, by nature of the abuse, closely akin to Navajos just across the river. Driven by necessity to find protection and sanctuary with one another, a close symbolic relationship developed between these peoples.

To the south, along the courses of the upper Gila and Little Colorado River, Navajos frequently consorted with Gileño Apaches. In the mid-1830s Chihuahua and Sonora put into effect against Apaches, a plan similar to that utilized by New Mexico against Navajos. To intimidate Apaches, who were raiding nearly to the Tropic of Cancer, a bounty was offered for each Indian scalp—whether it be male or female. Plagued by scalp hunters, many Apache groups cemented friendships with Navajos, who were likewise dodging slave raiders. It was during this period that head chief of the Gila Apaches, Mangas Coloradas, married one of his daughters to a Navajo headman, thus securing Navajos as allies in his wars against Mexicans. The solidarity of this unwritten bond of aid has been demonstrated numerous times. A Mexican military expedition in 1838 pursued a group of Navajos to the Gila River; where Apaches united with their cousins, and attacked viciously the pursuers.[28] And Apache country, at the headwaters of the Gila, was utilized by Navajos as a springboard for attacks against Socorro, and Limitar; and many tribesmen may have joined Apaches in their forays into the heart of Mexico.

The years between the worthless treaty of 1841 until 1846 were troublous times for New Mexico. Although there was another incipient peace treaty enacted with Navajos in 1844, the Mexican government was totally unable to deal with these Indians. All it could do was put up a semblance of defense—and those *caballeros* of the frontier, the slave raiders and scalp hunters, were the natural product of this period. And the laments of the New Mexican governor and his officials, who complained that "the war with the Navajos is slowly consuming the department," indeed rings true. It was the natural consequence of the now very profitable slave trade.[29]

* * *

1. For tabulations as to number of Navajos baptized in churches throughout New Mexico consult: David M. Brugge, "Causes of the Navajo Wars," *Navajo Times* (Vol. 6, June 1965); also Brugge's excellent account, "Some Plains Indians in the Church Records of New Mexico," *Plains Anthropologist* (Oct. 1965), pp. 181-89.

2. Frank Reeve, "The Navaho-Spanish Peace 1720s-1770s," *New Mexico Historical Review* (Vol. XXXIII, January 1959), p. 29.

3. Reeve, "Navaho-Spanish Diplomacy, 1770-1790," *Ibid.* (Vol. XXXV, July 1960), p. 200.

4. *Ibid.*, p. 219.

5. See Wesley R. Hurt, Jr., "Eighteenth Century Navaho Hogans from Canyon de Chelly National Monument," *American Antiquity* (Vol. VIII, July 1942), pp. 99.

6. Extracts of Records of Missions of San Esteban de Acoma and San José de la Laguna, selected by J. Lee Correll and David M. Brugge; on file with Navajo Land Claims Department, Window Rock, Arizona. A copy of these translations is also on file at the Arizona Pioneers' Historical Society, Tucson.

7. Chronological Tabulation & Summary of Baptismals, accompanying *ibid.*

8. See Hurt, *op. cit.* for additional details.

9. For details of the war of 1804-05, consult the correspondence of Salcedo to Chacon, September 16, 1804; Narbona to Chacon, December 10, 1804 (Documents Nos. 1754, 1778 and 1792), all in New Mexico Record Center and Archives, Santa Fe. Hereafter cited as NMSRCA.

10. A microfilm copy of the Records of the Arizpe Parish is

on file with the Special Collections, Western Division, University Library, University of Arizona.

11. Henri Folmer, "Contraband Trade between Louisiana and New Mexico in the Eighteenth Century," *New Mexico Historical Review* (Vol. XVI, July 1941).

12. For additional details bearing upon establishment of Comanche-Spanish economic ties see: Alfred B. Thomas (ed. & trans.), *Forgotten Frontiers, a Study of Spanish Indian Policy of Don Juan Bautista de Anza* (Norman: University of Oklahoma Press, 1932).

13. As quoted in Eleanor B. Adams & Angelico Chavez (eds.), *The Missions of New Mexico* (Albuquerque: University of New Mexico Press, 1956), pp. 252-253.

14. Facundo to First Alcalde of Santa Fe, April 24, 1822; NMSRCA.

15. Alejo Garcia Conde to Melgares, June 15, 1822; Records of New Mexico Junta Provincial, Santa Fe, April 26, 1822; NMSRCA.

16. Copy of peace treaty with Navajos and terms thereof, and recommendations of Governor Jos. Antonio Vizcarra, February 5, 1823; NMSRCA.

17. Record of meeting between Vizcarra and Navajo Tribe, February 12, 1823; Plan of war is an enclosure of the above document. All in NMSRCA.

18. David M. Brugge (ed.), "Vizcarra's Navajo Campaign of 1823," *Arizona & the West* (Vol. VI, Autumn 1964).

19. Reports of Vizcarra to Illustrious Municipal Government of Santa Fe, June 17, 1823, January 16, 1824; NMSRCA.

20. This data was taken from a tabulation of baptismals prepared by David M. Brugge, for a paper delivered at the 1965 Ethnohistorical Conference, Tucson, Arizona.

21. Vizcarra's treaty was caught in bureaucratic red tape and never shows ratification by Supreme Government of Mexico. See Gaspar de Ochoa to Comandante General of New Mexico, April 6, 1824; NMSRCA.

22. Record Book of Comandancia General, Santa Fe, copy of Report to Comandante General Inspector, October 15, 1832; *Ibid.*

23. Entry No. 67 of Record Book of Letters sent to Comandante General [Chihuahua], by Governor of New Mexico; in *ibid.*

24. See correspondence of Francisco Sandoval, Commander of Rurales & Justice of the Frontier of Jemez to Inhabitants of New Mexico, July 1839; *ibid.*

25. A campaign against Navajo in the Cañon de Chelly and Black Mesa area was conducted during October to December 1839. At the same time Don Juan Ramirez, with sixty men

from Cebolleta, marched against Navajos residing at Laguna Colorado. Two other campaigns were also launched, one commanded by José Salazar, and the other by Don José Francisco Vigil. See Governor's Letter Book for Year 1840, in *ibid*.

26. Copy of Treaty of March 10, 1841 in *ibid*.

27. Juan Andres Archuleta to Governor and Comandante General of Department, March 12, 1841; in *ibid*.

28. Letterbook of Comandencia General, November 25, 1838; *ibid*.

29. Armijo to Prefect of District of the Southwest, in Governor's Letterbook, April 28, 1846; *ibid*.

II

In mid-August 1846 Brigadier General Stephen Watts
Kearny took possession of New Mexico in the name of
the United States. Assuming the role of protector, the
Anglo commandant assured the conquered populace
that his government was aware of at least one of the
many difficulties which had plagued the area for
generations:

> The Apaches and the Navajos come down from
> the mountains and carry off your sheep and your
> women whenever they please. My government will
> correct all this. They will keep off the Indians,
> protect you in your persons and property.[1]

The fulfillment of General Kearny's promise of protection was not to be an easy task, for he and subsequent American administrators had little understanding
of the roots of the problems. Hostilities arising from
the reciprocal slave raids would remain a major source
of irritation confronting military and civil authorities

during the first two decades of United States occupation.[2]

To fulfill his promise of protection for the territory, General Kearny instructed his subordinate, the elected colonel of the First Regiment of Missouri Volunteers, Alexander W. Doniphan, to turn his attention to the Navajo menace. A rapid encircling movement of the tribe's domain was made, followed by a treaty on November 22, 1846 at Ojo del Oso (Bear Springs), on the north slopes of the Zuñi Mountains, fifteen miles east of present-day Gallup, New Mexico. During the negotiations Doniphan gently rebuked the Diné for their constant raiding. He explained that although the United States was at war with the Mexicans, he was still obligated to protect them.[3] This first treaty had little effect upon Navajos and served only to form an acquaintance between the Anglo-Americans and the Indians. As yet the Diné had no concept of United States military strength; and because protection had been extended to New Mexicans—for whom Navajos held only enmity—the weakness of the former regime was associated with that of the newcomers. To Navajos the change in New Mexican government mattered little. Resentment ran deep for the slave raids perpetrated against the tribe during the 1830s and 1840s; and small war parties frequently stole through passes of the Chuska-Tunicha Mountains and along well-beaten trails of the Zuñi Mountains. Down the Valley of the Rio San José, and through the wide, sandy valley of the Rio Puerco of the East, the Diné crept on their pilfering expeditions. In the late months of 1846, sheep and horses running into tens of thousands were driven from New Mexican ranches by illusive Indians. Try as it might, the United States military was powerless against these swiftly moving raiders. Doniphan's expedition and his overtures of peace to the Navajos had been in vain.

The sustained hostilities had a profound effect upon the attitudes of the New Mexican people, who were clamoring for the suppression of Navajo incursions. As during the Spanish period, as well as that of the Mexican, plans would be formulated—many for personal gain—ranging from total annihilation of the tribe to virtual enslavement of it. On every occasion New Mexican lawmakers pressed the army to undertake the task of subduing the Indians. But regiments, during those early years, were few and widely scattered in garrison duty—leaving the arid southwest unprotected. Frontier towns such as Abiquiu, Cubero, Cebolleta, Socorro, and the pueblos of Jemez, Santo Domingo and Zuñi were struck at repeatedly by Navajos. To alleviate their beleagured condition, inhabitants of these and other towns frequently organized reprisal expeditions against the Diné—usually without official army sanction.

A detailed report submitted by a Ramon Luna, Prefect of the County of Valencia, to the territorial Secretary of State, is illustrative of the utter ineffectuality of the United States troops garrisoned in New Mexico during the initial years of Anglo-American occupation —as well as the range and inevitable results of such volunteer campaigns:

Under date of 16th November last [1850] I received a communication from Mesrs. Andres Romero and Anastacio Garcia, citizens of the country under my jurisdiction, informing me that the Navajos had robbed them of 2000 sheep at the point called Valverde. I immediately issued orders to the alcaldes of the county to collect the best men they could find, and be ready at . . . Cubero on the following day, while I proceeded to Cebolleta, to demand assistance from the commander of the troops stationed at that point, which I effected immediately on my arrival through a despatch asking him for the mentioned assistance . . . He returned me a verbal answer that he would not give me the assistance . . ., as the horses belonging to the troops were in a wild state. From these

[Cebolleta] I was obliged to proceed with only fourteen men . . . furnished to me by the alcaldes . . . I was, [however], reinforced by forty men forming part of a volunteer company which was being raised at that time by permission of the commander . . . at Cebolleta; and which were going on an expedition to the Navajo country. With this reinforcement I proceeded to the vicinity of Colorado Lake, where we joined the balance of the volunteer company. There, we succeeded in capturing 500 of the stolen sheep. Finding myself at this point, it was impossible for me to return with so small a number of sheep. I therefore went on . . . to "Mesa de la Vaca" [Black Mesa], there I divided my forces and scattered them on various routes to the Navajo country. I succeeded in chastising the Indians and taking . . . stock amounting to 500 sheep, 150 riding animals, 11 oxen and 28 [female] prisoners, also 24 [males] . . .[4]

Although these independent forays were extremely hazardous, they could, as Luna's report hints at, be very profitable. The captors of Navajo women and children often gained dividends from their sale as menials to New Mexican householders, for as one early-day resident of Cebolleta recalled, "taking some [Navajo] man or woman captive . . . was one of the greatest rewards of a campaign, depending upon whether they were lucky with the captive whom they risked their lives in taking. If the captives were of average age, or young and could be domesticated and taught, then their captors bore rich fruits.[5] Regardless of how rewarding these volunteer excursions were, they invariably incited the Navajos to greater hostilities.

*   *   *

On July 22, 1849, James S. Calhoun[6] arrived in Santa Fe to assume the duties of Indian Agent for New

Mexico. He was directed by the Commissioner of Indian Affairs, William Medill, to gather data that would lead to an intelligent understanding of the Indian problems of that region. Calhoun plunged into the task of administering the affairs of peaceful tribes and suppressing hostile ones. Faced with the halting of Navajo depredations, he sought council with headmen of the tribe, and went to work through a continual correspondence with the Commissioner of Indian Affairs and the Secretary of War to gain adequate protection for the New Mexican frontier. The new Indian agent sought official establishment of a militia which could be on call at a moment's notice. However, Calhoun's movement for organization of irregular companies would add impetus to the Indian slave traffic—a traffic which would cease only when national attention had been focused upon it.

On July 19, 1851, Colonel Edwin V. Sumner[7] assumed command of the newly established Ninth Military Department—a jurisdiction which included virtually all of the present-day states of Arizona and New Mexico. Sumner was instructed by the Secretary of War to cooperate with Calhoun—who by now was Governor and Superintendent of Indian Affairs—in all matters dealing with the Indians. Despite this order, Sumner and Calhoun soon disagreed violently on points of major policy. Two weeks after assumption of governorship, Calhoun issued a proclamation authorizing raising of volunteer companies to campaign against Apache and Navajo Indians.[8] The manner in which the governor proposed to pay these "volunteers" gave the slave raiders an "open season" upon any and all Indians:

> I further direct and order that the property which may be captured from any hostile tribe of Indians, by any company raised under the foregoing provisions, shall be disposed of in accordance with the laws and customs heretofore existing in this terri-

tory—until legislative action shall be had upon the subject, either by the Congress of the United States the Legislative Assembly of the Territory.[9]

More than a decade would pass before congressional action would be taken to alter this proclamation—and disposal of captured "property" would continue in the traditional manner. Calhoun's "volunteers" would be first of many sanctioned militia groups to range Navajo country, raking in a profitable harvest of captives and livestock—and inciting the Indians to greater depredations.

With publication of Governor Calhoun's proclamation came a flood of applications to raise and arm militia companies. From the northern and more exposed New Mexican counties of Taos and Rio Arriba, pressure was brought to bear upon the Territorial Legislature for large scale organization of militia. On July 20, 1851, the governor was presented with a petition prepared by territorial representatives enumerating the great loss of property occasioned by Navajo forays. This document, besides expanding the activities of irregular military forces, offered enticing compensation —additional volunteer companies would be raised at no additional cost to the already strained territorial budget. According to this request, the militia, armed with weapons furnished from regular army stores, would not receive their pay from territorial funds or from regular army appropriations, but instead would share equally "all the captives, and other spoils that may be taken."[10]

When this petition was passed on to Colonel Sumner, he clearly saw that here was one of the sources of Indian troubles which had plagued New Mexico for generations. Volunteers had habitually made forays against the Navajos. In a far-sighted manner Sumner felt that if hostilities were to be halted, private incursions must be restrained, and Navajos put under the surveillance of the regular army—both for their own protection as well as for that of the Mexican and Anglo population of New Mexico.

Sumner's hands, however, were tied by instructions from the War Department, advising him to work in close accord with civil authority. Thus he could only accede to the request for arms—but with reservations. The weapons issued to volunteers would be subject to recall by the commanding officer of the Ninth Military Department, and were never to be used in hostile forays into Indian country unless the militia was acting in conjunction with regular troops. Needless to say, these stipulations produced an unfavorable reaction among those who did not wish to be restricted in their raids against the Navajos.[11]

Not only were New Mexicans endeavoring to gain official sanction for their raids, but other Indians were anxious to strike the Diné. The pueblos of Zuñi and Jemez—both targets of Navajo aggression—sought arms and assent from United States authorities. Even among the Navajos themselves certain individuals were seeking gain by attacking their own brethren. A band of renegades, known to their tribesmen as *Diné 'ana-ih* (Enemy Navajos), who had long resided in the vicinity of Cebolleta, constantly allied themselves with New Mexicans during the conduct of reprisal expeditions. This band and its leader, Antonio Sandoval,[12] had for a number of years maintained friendly relations with the frontier settlements of Cubero and Cebolleta; and had used this favored position to barter Navajo prisoners captured from more recalcitrant bands. It was because of his participation in the lucrative slave trade, and his outward demonstration of friendship toward the Navajos' sworn enemies, that Sandoval was held in disrepute by his own tribesmen.

Sandoval's role as slave-raider is highlighted in many reports by military men and early-day travelers; and he was without a doubt the leading participant in the trade in New Mexico. The Reverend Hiram Read, Baptist missionary, while visiting Cebolleta, described the chief's activities of March 11, 1851, in these terse words:

> A famous half-tamed Navajo Chief named San-doval who resides in this vicinity, came into town today to sell some captives of his own nation which he has recently took prisoners. He sold one young man of 18 years of age for thirty (30) dollars.[13]

The great vigor with which Sandoval pursued his profession was pointed out in a letter by Governor Calhoun to Commissioner of Indian Affairs, Luke Lea (dated March 31, 1851):

> Sandoval, our Navajo friend near Cebolleta, returned about the 20th of the month from a visit to his brethren with eighteen captives, a quantity of stock and several scalps.[14]

*   *   *

Not only did reprisal expeditions pose a problem, but the wandering merchant frequently assumed the role of slave raider. Numerous traders penetrated Indian country, and their clandestine operations were difficult to control, and served to agitate the Indian. These individuals, "who would sell their kith and kin," reaped enormous profits from sale of the human commodity. The frontier towns of Abiquiu, Cebolleta and Cubero were now the established rendezvous for unscrupulous merchants, whose range was the whole extent of Navajoland, and even beyond.[15] Traders of human flesh were always anxious to keep hostilities alive between the Government of the United States and the Navajos—for then they could readily gain official sanction to assume the role of "volunteers"—their compensation being permission to keep and dispose of, as they saw fit, all Navajo women and children captured during their campaigns.

90

It seems almost ironic, that while James Calhoun, on one hand was furthering endeavors of slave raiders by urging formation of a militia, he was on the other hand, attempting to suppress the activities of slave traders. Indian Agent Calhoun often wrote of the evils inherent in the clandestine traffic, and even took measures to regulate it, as indicated in a letter penned to the Commissioner of Indian Affairs. In this communication the agent stated that "the constant and unrestrained intercourse of traders with the Indians of this territory is, perhaps, the greatest curse upon it, and so exceedingly pernicious is it, I have ventured to suggest to Governor Munroe, the propriety of extending, *by order,* the laws of Congress in relation to trade and intercourse with Indians . . ."[16]

Apparently Calhoun's suggestion was taken seriously by the Military Governor of New Mexico, for on November 21, 1849, the following notice was publicly displayed at Santa Fe:

Licenses to trade with Indians, will be granted by the undersigned, upon the following conditions, provided they are approved by his excellency, Governor Munroe, Military commander of this Department.

Applicants must be citizens of the United States, produce satisfactory testimonials of good character, and give bond in a penal sum not *exceeding* five thousand dollars, with one or more sureties, that he will faithfully observe all the laws and regulations made for the government of trade and intercourse with the Indian tribes of the United States, and in no respect violate the same, and that they will not trade in firearms, powder, lead, or other munitions of war.

Applicants will distinctly state what tribe they wish to trade with, and under a license granted, they will not be authorized to trade with others.

For the present, no license will be granted

authoring trade or intercourse with the Apaches, Navajos, or Utahs.

(Signed) JAMES S. CALHOUN, *Indian Agent*

Most traders adhered strictly to the stipulations of their permits, but there were others who went far afield on licenses granted by Calhoun and Governor Munroe, to barter weapons, shot and powder for Indian captives. Into Utah and Mormon territory, went men such as Pedro León, seeking women and children among Utes and Paiutes. And to northern Sonora and Chihuahua, went Peter Blacklaws, and others to glean captives from Comanches, Kiowas and Apaches returning from raids deep into interior Mexico.

It was not difficult to circumvent trade restrictions when there were little if any means to enforce them. Methods employed to get around Indian intercourse laws were indeed varied. Often one permit would be used by scores of New Mexicans, the original holder sub-leasing, so to speak, his rights to barter among Indians.[18] Still other traders would seek permits to operate among peaceful tribes, such as Puebloans and Paiute groups; and then when beyond all means of surveillance, head directly for Ute, Apache or Navajo country—where captives in quantity awaited exchange for arms, powder, lead, and that rotgut liquor known as "Taos Lightning."

It was little wonder, during the initial years of Anglo-American occupation of the southwest, that this area was "a dark and bloody ground." Constant raids by slave procurers kept tribes in a state of agitation, and the clandestine operations of traders, bartering arms and whiskey for captives, kept more mobile tribes upon the plunder trails.

*   *   *

Regardless of repeated inroads by New Mexican slave raiders, and the commerce of Indian traders, by spring 1852 Navajos were at last demonstrating a desire for peace. The relaxation of raids was due, no doubt, to the establishment of Fort Defiance in September of 1851.[14] But many incidents involving the pursuers struck directly into Navajo country, and attaking of captives occurred between Navajos and New Mexicans—which threatened to erupt into open warfare. One such incident took place on the night of May 3, 1853. A sheep owner, named Ramón Martín, his two sons, María and Librado and four herders, were watching over their flock near Chamas, when, from out of the underbrush a volley of shots brought down Señor Martín—mortally wounded. Mariá, upon seeing his father shot, ran for cover and hid until morning. From his place of concealment, the boy watched four Navajos approach the sheep pen and round up his brother and the four other shepherds, as another Indian secured the horses. Each youth was then roped about the neck, and led away for about a quarter of a mile to a watering place. Three of the captives were then set free and told in broken Spanish to return and inform their people that when the Mexicans gave up a paint horse and a mule stolen from the Navajos, and the animals returned to their owners, the two captive boys would be given up. With delivery of these words, the Navajos rode off with Librado and the other boy.[20]

Informed of the murder of Martín and the kidnapping of the two boys, Governor William Carr Lane immediately recognized the danger inherent in the explosive situation, and ordered Donaciaro Vigil, Territorial Secretary, and a man thoroughly familiar with Navajos, to ascertain the identity of the murderers. At the same time he was to proclaim to the tribe that failure to give up the culprits and captives would be considered a justifiable cause of war.[21] In compliance with the governor's orders, Vigil proceeded to Navajo country, and parlayed with Chiefs Armijo and Aguila Negra on May 17. Upon receipt of the governor's ultimatum, the Indians released the two boys, and promised to cooperate in the apprehension of the malefactors.[22] Fortunately for New Mexico, the tensions eased, and a period of watchful co-existence followed.

Not only were Navajos intimidated by a military garrison in their country, but they were held in check by the constant threat which the army reiterated—that unless the Indians kept the peace "the Mexicans, the Pueblos, Sandoval's people and the Americans would be let loose upon them, their flocks seized, their men killed; their women and children taken prisoners." That the commanding officer of the new post in Navajoland, Captain Henry Lane Kendrick, was an advocate of this peace-keeping method is exemplified in a letter to the assistant adjutant general of New Mexico, in which he stated:

> I feel constrained to say that the most efficient rod in terrorem (sic) to be held over these people is the fear of a permission being given to the Mexicans to make captives of Navajos and to retain them, a permission at once wise and philanthropic and one which would at an early date settle the question.[23]

By 1857, however, Kendrick's "wise and philanthropic" solution to the Navajo problem was beginning to break down, and war finally erupted in 1858—due in large measure to the insidious activities of slave raiders.

In February of that year Indians were put in a belligerent mood by an attack by New Mexicans upon a peaceful band of Navajos near Albuquerque. The following month, Navajos were again attacked by another party of New Mexicans and Utes, who set out from Abiquiu in pursuit of animals believed stolen by Navajos. Instead of following the trail left by the thieves, the pursuers struck directly into Navajo country, and attacked the first party of Indians encountered. As usual New Mexicans redeemed their losses by taking captives, who were sold upon the party's return to Abiquiu.[24] The real war, however, broke out at Fort Defiance and was precipitated indirectly by the usual cause—slaves. On July 12, 1858, a Negro servant belonging to post commandant, Major Thomas H. Brooks, was slain by a Navajo, and surrender of the murderer was demanded of Chief Zarcillas Largos. Instead, the Indian suggested that traditional blood money be paid. This did not satisfy Major Brooks, and he gave the Navajos twenty days in which to produce the killer. The Diné attempted to deceive the major by presenting him with the body of a Mexican captive. The major denied that the corpse was that of the culprit—and this was an insult to Navajo integrity, and considered by them as a provocation for war.

Hostilities began in August, and from then until December Navajo country was scoured by military expeditions. Corn fields were burned, hogans demolished, and hostiles sent retreating for safety of the more inaccessible areas of their homeland. Destructive as these military movements may have been, raids by the Navajo's mortal enemies, the Utes, were the most devastating. Armed with the finest rifles procurable, and with ammunition doled from the very hands of their agent at Abiquiu, these Indians struck repeatedly during late months of 1858.

Although the number of reports pertaining to official sanctioning of Ute raiding is large, the rewards offered these Indians by government agents were always lightly skipped over—or not mentioned at all. Only in the few documents which tell of the outcome of these raids, do we see how Utes were paid, for as Colonel Dixon Miles, commanding United States troops in Navajoland, wrote on November 23, 1858: "eight days since a large force of Utahs attacked the band of Caballado Mucho, on the San Juan opposite (north) of the Carrizo Mountains, killing ten Navajos, capturing six women and children and their whole herd of horses."[25] On December 18, Albert W. Pheiffer, Ute agent at Abiquiu, wrote of his charges' movements: "two days ago most of the warriors of the Muatches (between 50 to 60) were here to make a campaign against the Navajos. Some Apaches under Fletcho Bayeda joined them here, and also some Capotes. They staid a day and a half at the agency, and then they went. I thought best to let them go, if they wanted to . . . They expected a large Mexican force to join them from Taos and vicinity." Ten days later came the results of this war party's activities—and successful they were. ". . . the Utes returned on Monday with eighteen ponys. The first party killed two Navajos and brought [in] two children. And all the rest returned on Tuesday, bringing in all, twenty-one little girls and from fifty to seventy-five ponys."[26]

It was little wonder therefore, that Navajos fearful for the safety of their families and livestock, abandoned portions of their homeland that lay within easy reach of Ute and New Mexican raiders. Tribesmen residing within fifty miles of the Rio San Juan, the stream separating Navajoland from Ute domain, abandoned grazing and planting grounds to seek sanctuary in the deeper recesses of their homeland.

As the Bonneville Treaty, which concluded the war of 1858, rigidly defined limits of Navajo country, as well as drastically reduced the tribe's domain, it was a provocative cause for renewal of the depredations during early 1859. So too, was it natural for the cry to arise from New Mexico's populace for adequate protection. As always, the regular army, equipped with grain fed and coddled horses, were powerless against swiftly moving Indians. Again, the militia law of 1851—the very same one passed by Governor James Calhoun—was invoked. This time it was Governor Abraham Rencher who was spokesman; and his amendments to the law encouraged slave raiding to a far greater extent:

Be it enacted by the Legislative Assembly of the Territory of New Mexico:

That any man of experience and good character who shall raise and organize a force of not less than two hundred men nor more than two hundred and twenty-five men is hereby authorized to apply to the governor of this territory to make a volunteer campaign against any tribe or tribes of Indians at war with this territory . . ."[27]

Six months later Navajo country was again in the throes of war; and the rincons of the Chuska-Tunicha Mountains were scoured for Indian camps by slave raiding militia. In mid-June a party of 300 men, organized by Ramón Baca of Cebolleta, penetrated Navajoland. By first week of July, this group had thoroughly scouted the mountains east of Fort Defiance; and succeeded in capturing 2000 sheep, 50 horses, and fourteen women and children, who, fettered, were carried to Cebolleta and there sold into bondage.[28] Not all volunteer expeditions were as lucky as Baca's, however. Late in June a party of eighty New Mexicans were surprised by Navajos in Chuska Valley. They lost thirty killed, and thirteen wounded—and the survivors were indeed lucky to make their way back to Fort Defiance.[29]

Throughout the latter months of 1860, one military expedition after another criss-crossed Navajoland; and numerous groups of New Mexicans, Utes, Puebloans and Apaches descended upon the Navajos. By February 1861 tribesmen had had enough, and sued for peace. On the 15th of that month another treaty was signed between thirty-two headmen and Colonel R.E.S. Canby, commanding the Ango-American military. So impoverished and beaten did Navajos appear, that military leaders felt confident that a lasting peace had finally been concluded. In fact, both Canby and department commander, Colonel Thomas T. Fauntleroy, deemed the peace lasting enough to order abandonment of Fort Defiance. Throughout spring materiel and troops were transferred from Cañon Bonito to a new post being erected on the slopes of the Zuñi Mountains—Fort Fauntleroy. Finally, on April 25, 1861, the last troops were withdrawn from Fort Defiance.[30]

Abandonment of Fort Defiance and reduction of troops in Navajoland were perhaps too hasty, for influences were at work—many traditional—which would never allow a lasting peace. As always there was that element among New Mexico's population that overlooked any treaty of peace between Navajos and the United States Government. The slave raiders were again on the prowl. The ink on Canby's Treaty had scarcely dried before a party of thirty-one New Mexicans from Taos were apprehended by military patrols—with six bound Navajo squaws in their possession. These slave raiders proudly admitted killing one man and six women and children before obtaining their captives. But most important of all, was the fact that this party demonstrated the feeling prevalent in New Mexico's settlements, when they "openly avowed their intentions to disregard the treaty . . ., and on their return home, to organize a new expedition to capture Navajos and sell them [on the Rio Grande]."

If these disruptive incidents were the work of just a few lawless individuals, they could have been quickly and efficiently dealt with by the military. The magnitude and organization of the slave raids, however, made it virtually impossible for the army to protect the Navajo. Throughout March large scale inroads were made by New Mexicans. The band of Ganado Mucho —always the friend of Anglo-Americans—was attacked, and fifty of its horses stolen. Fifteen Navajo rancherías belonging to the bands of Herrero Grande, Vincente Baca and El Chapador were also attacked by raiders, probably from Cubero and Cebolleta.[31]

Colonel Canby quickly realized how devastating these wanton acts were to peace with tribesmen, for on

February 27 he wrote to department commander T. T. Fauntleroy:

> These and other occurrences of minor importance indicate, I think, a settled disposition on the part of some of these people to protract the Navajo troubles indefinitely.

* * *

> For myself I shall have no hesitation in treating as enemies of the United States any parties of Mexicans or Pueblo Indians who may be found assigned to the Navajos.[32]

Colonel Canby, however, was destined never to have the opportunity to take the measures he deemed necessary for securement of peace with the Navajos. Far to the east and south of New Mexico another conflict of greater magnitude was gathering. With election of Abraham Lincoln to the presidency, the question of slavery—although of a different type—was brought finally to a head. Throughout January 1861, one southern state after another declared its independence—South Carolina, Mississippi, Florida, Alabama, Louisiana, Georgia; and on February 1—Texas. The Civil War was on.

* * *

1. George R. Gibson, *Journal of a Soldier Under Kearny and Doniphan*, 1846-47, edited by Ralph P. Bieber (Glendale: Arthur H. Clark, 1935), pp. 75-76.

2. For an idea of the role played by slave raiding in inciting western tribes consult: Joint Special Committee, *Condition of Tribes* (Washington 1867). This work is also known as the Doolittle Report.

3. John T. Hughes, *Doniphan's Expedition: Containing an Account of the Conquest of New Mexico* (Cincinnati: 1847), pp. 71-72.

4. Ramon Luna to Donaciano Vigil, January 20, 1851; in

Annie H. Abel (comp. & ed.), *Official Correspondence of James S. Calhoun while Indian Agent at Santa Fe and Superintendent of Indian Affairs* (Washington: 1915), pp. 285-86. Hereafter referred to as *Calhoun Correspondence*.

5. C. C. Marino, "The Seboyetanos and the Navahos," *New Mexico Historical Review* (Vol. XXIX, January 1954), p. 11.

6. James S. Calhoun, the first territorial governor of New Mexico was a staunch Whig, and professed a great admiration for General Zachary Taylor, which gained him a captaincy of a regiment of Georgia volunteers during the Mexican War. He served in this capacity from June until May 1847, at which time he was commissioned a lieutenant colonel commanding a battalion of Georgia volunteers. With the opening of President Taylor's administration, Calhoun received the appointment of United States Indian Agent at Santa Fe; and on March 3, 1851 was inaugurated as governor, assuming his duties as *ex officio* Superintendent of Indian Affairs for the territory. See *Calhoun Correspondence*.

7. Although not a West Point graduate, Edwin Vose Sumner was an eminent officer. He served throughout the Black Hawk War; and in 1833 entered the Second Dragoons, and began his services on the western frontier with the rank of captain. Sumner served with General Winfield Scott throughout the Mexican War, and was commissioned lieutenant colonel of the First Dragoons. From 1851 until 1853 he was commander of the Ninth Department, as well as serving a short term as governor of New Mexico. See R. E. Twitchell, *Leading Facts of New Mexican History* (Cedar Rapids: 1912), Vol. II, p. 286.

8. Proclamation (dated March 20, 1851); *Calhoun Correspondence*, pp. 300-305.

9. Proclamation "to the People of Said Territory," by James S. Calhoun (dated March 8, 1851); National Archives, New Mexico Territorial Papers, 1851-60. Hereafter cited as Territorial Papers.

10. *Calhoun Correspondence*, pp. 386-87.

11. *Ibid.*, p. 499.

12. Sandoval, known to his people as Hastin Késhgoli (Crooked Foot), was of the clan Tehedlíni, or Crossed Waters People. He and his son acted as guides for Doniphan's expedition—the first United States military expedition into Navajoland, as well as many subsequent ones. See Richard Van Valkenburgh, "Navajo Naataani," *The Kiva* (Vol. XIII, January 1948), p. 19.

13. Lansing P. Bloom (ed.), "The Rev. Hiram Read, Baptist Missionary to New Mexico," *New Mexico Historical Review* (Vol. XVII, April 1942), p. 133.

14. National Archives; Records of the Office of Indian Af-

fairs, New Mexico Superintendency Papers, Record Group 75, Letters Received. Hereafter cited as Superintendency Papers, LR.

15. Mormon missionary Daniel W. Jones demonstrated the widespread activities of New Mexican traders during 1851 with the following account: "the people of New Mexico . . . were making annual trips, commencing with a few goods, trading on their way with either Navajos or Utes (generally with the Navajos) for horses, which they sold very cheap . . . These used-up horses were brought through and traded to the poorer Indians for children. This was continued into Lower California, where the children . . . would be traded to the Mexican-Californians for other horses, goods or cash." Daniel W. Jones, *Forty Years Among the Indians* (Los Angeles, Westernlore Press, 1960), p. 47.

16. Calhoun to Orlando Brown, November 2, 1849; National Archives, Records of Office of Indian Affairs, Record Group 75, New Mexico Superintendency Records, Letters Received. Hereafter cited as Superintendency Records, LR.

17. In *Ibid.*

18. In mid-June 1850, Captain John Buford, commandant of the garrison at Cebolleta, apprehended a party of traders suspected of dealing in captives. The official report of this incident shows the great lengths at which traders would go in order to ply their commerce:

"At half past one o'clock p.m. [on June 15] . . . a report reached me that a large party of traders were in the vicinity of Acoma en route for the Apache and Navajo . . . I instantly ordered all the available men of Company H, Second Dragoons, to saddle up . . . On the 16th at 5 p.m. we [took] possession of the traders' camp which was about two miles southwest from Acoma.

"Juan Padilla of Atrisco was speaker for the party [numbering fifty-four] and his headman . . . He could produce no license to trade with any Indians whatever and said his intentions was to trade with the Zuñians only. The lie was given him by several of his party, who insisted upon his giving a true statement. This he refused to do. The statement of his party is that Juan Padilla said he had a license to trade with the Apaches and Navajos, and they had obtained licenses from him for the same purpose at the rate of $2 per man.

"A considerable amount of powder, lead was found in their packs of goods . . ." Buford to L. McLaws, June 19, 1850; National Archives, Records of United States Army Commands, Record Group 98, Department of New Mexico, Letters Received. Hereafter cited as Department of New Mexico, L.R.

19. Departmental Order No. 29 (dated September 19, 1851); in *ibid.*

20. John Grenier to W. C. Lane (n.d.); Superintendency Papers, L.R.

21. W. C. Lane to Donaciaro Vigil, May 9, 1853; *ibid.*

22. Annie H. Abel (ed.), "Indian Affairs Under the Administration of William Carr Lane," *New Mexico Historical Review* (Vol. XVI, July 1941), p. 341.

23. Wendrick to S. D. Sturgis, June 11, 1853; Department of New Mexico, LR.

24. John Ward to Samuel M. Yost, April 9, 1858; Superintendency Records, LR.

25. Miles to J. D. Wilkins, November 23, 1858; Department of New Mexico, LR.

26. Pheiffer to Collins, December 18, 1859, and Juan Valdez to Pheiffer, December 29, 1859; all in Superintendency Records, Letters Received from Agencies.

27. "An act Amendatory to the Militia Law of the Territory of New Mexico," (dated January 28, 1859); in Territorial Papers.

28. Santa Fe *Weekly Gazette,* July 18, 1860.

29. Collins to A. B. Greenwood, July 27, 1860; Superintendency Papers, LR.

30. Canby to A. A. G., March 11, 1861; Department of New Mexico, LR. Also National Archives, Records of the Office of Adjutant General, Record Group 94, Fort Defiance Post Returns, April 1861. Hereafter cited as Fort Defiance Post Returns.

31. Canby to A. A. G., February 27, March 11 and 18, 1861; Department of New Mexico, LR.

32. Canby to Fauntleroy, February 27, 1861; *ibid.*

III

With eruption of the Civil War conditions in New Mexico grew worse. The Comanches and Kiowas on the east, Apaches to the south and west, and Navajos in the north ran riot as posts were abandoned and officers and troops defected to the South. To this was added another menace: Texas Confederates under Brigadier General Henry H. Sibley were marching up the Rio Grande late in 1861, driving Union forces before them. During their brief occupation of the territory, the Texans came face-to-face with the Navajos, and their cousins—the Apaches—who made no distinction between soldiers in blue or gray. Sibley had been in the territory but a short time before he formulated a plan to end the Indian problem—legal enslavement of all hostile tribes.[1] The Confederates, however, were never to realize their plans for conquest of the desert southwest, nor the enslavement of its Indians. From out of the west marched a column of California Volunteers under command of Colonel James H. Carleton, and from the north came Colorado Volunteers led by Colonel John B. Slough, to crush the Texans at Glorieta Pass in February 1862. The Civil War had come and gone in New Mexico, but there the slavery issue was never to be settled by the victory of Northern principles over those of the South.

The Navajos and Mescalero Apaches realized that attentions of the army had been diverted to repelling the Confederate invasion, and they stepped up their depredations. But the threat from Texas soon passed, and Colonel James H. Carleton, veteran Indian fighter, and organizer of the "California Column," was able to launch his plans for pacification of the Indians. The First and Second Regiments of New Mexico Volunteers, organized to repel the southern invasion, were put under command of one of the territory's leading citizens—Colonel Christopher "Kit" Carson, who ruthlessly applied sword and torch to Indian country. The roundup of the Mescaleros began in January 1863, and the "Long Walk" of the Navajos, followed six months later. Both terminated at a disease ridden reservation upon the banks of the Pecos River in east-central New Mexico—the infamous Bosque Redondo.[2]

Certain unscrupulous individuals, realizing that the roundup of Navajos would end forever their slave trading activities, took this last opportunity to obtain a few more menials—with the blessings of the military—for Carleton had given his approval to organization of volunteer groups, many having considerable experience fighting Indians. During the Carleton campaign Navajo country was alive with New Mexicans seeking women and children, who were in many cases, snatched from groups of Indians making their way to Forts Wingate and Canby to surrender.[3] Companies of irregulars from the slave dealing centers of Cubero, Cebolleta and Abiquiu made frequent raids upon Navajos. One such company of volunteers, recruited by Ramón A. Baca of Cebolleta, was highly successful in their forays, for "they took hundreds of prisoners, who, as was the custom . . . were sold a domestics all over the territory, sometimes at very high prices."[4]

This was also a time when the implacable enemies of the Diné from across the Rio San Juan also struck. Kit

Carson reported large concentrations of Ute warriors ranging the red rock country between the Carrizo Mountains and the east entrance of Cañon de Chelly in search of captives. Carson sought to capitalize upon animosities which existed between the two tribes; and employed Utes as scouts and guides. These Indians, from the mountains north of the Rio San Juan, proved so expert at ferreting out their enemies that they soon earned the acclaim of their commander. In true mountain man fashion, Carson wanted to reward his Ute allies for "their continued zeal and activity" in the Navajo campaign, by permitting them to retain women and children. The "Rope Thrower," as the Indians called Kit, was firmly convinced that captives disposed of in this manner would be better off than at Bosque Redondo, as the Utes would sell them to Mexican families who would care for them—thus they "would cease to require any further attention on the part of the government." He also advocated distributing captive Navajos as servants to New Mexican families in order to break up "that collectiveness of interest as a tribe which they will retain if kept together" at the Bosque Redondo.[5]

Never in the history of Anglo-American Indian affairs had a military campaign been carried to such proportions. For over eighteen months the general populace of New Mexico, Pueblo Indians, Utes and Apaches were armed to carry war into Navajoland. Parties of Navajos coming into Forts Wingate and Canby to surrender were attacked by New Mexicans, who drove off their sheep, seized whatever silver ornaments and blankets they could, and carried off their women and children.[6]

Even Indians who trustingly put their faith in the army, and chose captivity at Bosque Redondo to freedom in their beloved red rock country, were not spared by slave procurers. Many a party of Navajos being transported—under military guard—to Fort Sumner were viciously attacked. Particularly those Indians, who for reasons of illness and exhaustion lagged behind

105

their party, were victims of ever-preying slave raiders. In early May 1864, Lieutenant D. W. Brocheim, an officer in charge of escorting Navajos to Bosque Redondo, reported upon the consequences befalling Indians who were left behind without adequate military guard:

I received information this morning [May 2, 1864] that a party of friendly Navajo Indians who had been with Captain McCabe en route to Fort Sumner having fallen sick and unable to travel were left behind by him in Tejas Cañon, east of [Albuquerque] . . . Yesterday about noon while traveling along the road in front of San Antonio, six Mexicans came out from the town and took thirteen prisoners (eight women and five children) and took them back into the town.[7]

By late spring Navajos were surrendering in such numbers that both General Carlton and Colonel Carson suspended active military operations against the tribe for fear of injury to parties of friendly Indians making their way into Forts Canby and Wingate. Relaxation by the military, however, did not deter activities of intinerant militia companies, who roamed Navajoland. In fact, so extensive were the forays by these independent parties, that they threatened the very success of the Navajo campaign, and raised the ire of military personnel. Incensed by the wanton acts of New Mexicans from Cebolleta, Cubero, Abiquiu, as well as from towns in southern Colorado, Colonel Christopher Carson, in mid-April 1864, suggested that measures be adopted to curtail "independent campaigns."

"Since active hostilities have ceased against the Navajos," wrote the old scout, "various parties of citizens have come into their country for the purpose of robbing from the Navajos, and some of them have the audacity to steal from them under my protection at this post [Fort Canby].

"To counteract and put a stop to this state of affairs, which if continued would prevent the chiefs and others of their tribe from coming in with their stock, and complying with the instructions of the Department Commander, I would by leave respectfully suggest that Lieutenant Charles M. Hubbell, First Cavalry New Mexico Volunteers, with a party of enlisted men now on detached service at Los Piños be ordered forthwith, together with fifty (50) good serviceable horses, to join the regiment at Headquarters, to pursue and capture whatever bands of citizen marauders may come here for the purpose of thwarting the laudable actions of the government . . ."[8]

Apparently even members of the regiments of New Mexico Volunteers—the very units commanded by Carson—were not above abducting and selling Indian children now and then. On February 19, 1864, General Carleton's aide-de-camp, Cyrus H. DeForrest, wrote to the commandant of Fort Craig, that out of a party of twenty-two Navajos brought in by New Mexico Volunteers, there was missing a girl of seventeen years of age, named Guadalupe, who it was alleged, was sold to one Gregorio Sedallio, of Paraje.[9]

As the army was virtually powerless to stop this cruel and malicious practice, General Carleton sought aid from Governor Henry Connelly. In council, the two leaders discussed this insidious commerce, which had reached disgraceful proportions under their very guidance and sanction. Both men agreed to an immediate cessation of war against the Navajos, and the publication of a proclamation aimed at halting all forays by independent companies of civilians:

Whereas a suspension of arms, in the prosecution of the war against the Navajo tribe of Indians, exists, as the more hostile part of that tribe is now reduced to and located upon the reservation at the Bosque Redondo, and the remainder

107

of the tribe coming in and surrendering themselves to the military authorities; and

Whereas any hostile demonstrations upon the part of our citizens towards the said Indians during this suspension of hostilities would frustrate the intention sand efforts of the government in the peaceable removal of the remainder of this tribe, now collecting around Forts Canby and Wingate, to whom has been granted safety to life and property while there and *in transitu* to the reservation: Therefore,

I, Henry Connelly, governor of New Mexico, do issue this my proclamation, and ordain:

First. That hostilities on the part of the citizens with the remainder of the Navajo tribe of Indians, who have or have not presented themselves at the military posts for removal to the reservation, shall cease.

Second. That all forays by our citizens of a hostile character into the country heretofore or now occupied by any part of the said Navajo tribe of Indians, are hereby positively prohibited under the severest penalties.

Third. That any parties of armed men, with hostile intentions, hereafter found in the Navajo country, will be immediately arrested by the United States troops and sent to the headquarters of the department of New Mexico, here to be dealt with according to law.

Fourth. It is proper in this connexion to warn the people against further traffic in captive Indians. The laws of the country as well as those of justice and humanity positively forbid such a traffic. Measures are now being taken by the Department of Interior to have all Indians surrendered who have been sold into slavery, and the people therefore have this timely warning to refrain at once from any such traffic in Indian captives as has heretofore been practiced among them.

Done at Santa Fe, this 4th day of May, 1864.

(*Signed*) HENRY CONNELLY,

Governor and Commander[20]-in-
Chief of the Militia.

The publication of Governor Connelly's proclamation fell upon deaf ears. Now was the chance New Mexicans had waited for. The populace of the territory had groaned for generations under lightning-fast incursions of Navajos and Apaches. Livestock losses had been unbearably heavy, and settlements had been of necessity confined to the river valleys of New Mexico —the Rio Grande and Rio Puerco. At last the Navajos, as a tribe, had been hit hard by Kit Carson and his scorched earth policy. No proclamation—no matter how stringent—would halt New Mexicans from striking their mortal enemies. And no "laws of the country, as well as those of justice and humanity" would halt the traffic in Navajo captives.

Throughout spring and summer of 1865, the general populace of New Mexico, the Pueblo Indians, and Utes, prepared for war. The military commandants at Fort Wingate, Los Piños and Albuquerque were constantly approached for permission to raid the Navajos. From those villages, always notorious for their participation in illegal trade, came the itinerant militia captains, begging arms, ammunition, and assent to raid— the only recompense being retention of all booty taken from Indians.

Regardless of all proclamations prohibiting campaigns by militia, and the threats of immediate arrest of those who disregarded Governor Connelly's words, many United States military commanders shut their eyes to these itinerant groups. On May 13 Antonio Mejicano, "a citizen of Cubero," and two other Mexicans (names not specified) with 75 to 100 Zuñi Indians, applied for and received permission from Lieutenant Colonel Julius C. Shaw, commanding Fort Wingate, to campaign against Navajos.[11] One month later fifty volunteers, raised at Abiquiu, penetrated Indian country as far as the San Francisco Peaks, near present-day Flagstaff, Arizona.[12] Even Indian agents were doling out powder, lead and percussion caps to the Utes, so that this mountain tribe could successfully raid Navajos south of the Rio San Juan.[13] So the insidious activities of slave procurers continued, bringing death, destruction, and captivity to those of the Diné who had not surrendered and been transported to Bosque Redondo.

Although these raiders—even when officially sanctioned—were technically required to turn over all prisoners to the regular army, for transferral to the Navajo reservation, few if any did so—as verified by military correspondence. In a letter (dated May 25, 1865) Lieutenant Colonel Shaw admitted giving permission to Antonio Mejicano to retain five Navajo women, whose fate was readily apparent.[14] Testimony of Navajos fortunate enough to have either escaped or to have been released from captivity, seems to bear this out. A niece of the prominent chief, Herrero, recounted before a military court of enquiry, the circumstances of her abduction:

Question: Where were you taken prisoner?
Answer: At Casa Blanca near Moqui.
Question: Who took you prisoner?
Answer: An armed party of Mexicans from Cebolleta, who attacked our camp at day break, killed seven men and took twelve women and children prisoners.
Question: Where are the others who were taken the same time with yourself?
Answer: My two sisters were taken and sold at the Ranchos of Atrisco, and I heard that the others have been sold near Isleta or below the river.[15]

The vicious attacks by New Mexicans and their Pueblo and Ute allies continued throughout the remaining months of 1865 and into the following year. Navajos, however, were becoming more and more wary. In the rugged and extremely dissected country around Navajo Mountain they sought sanctuary from their enemies. Conserving their few remaining sheep and horses, the Indians grubbed a pitiful livelihood on wild potatoes and berries, and remained ever vigilant. Ute war parties and militia companies found fewer Navajo rancherías occupied; and those Indians unlucky enough to be surprised, resisted vigorously. A great number of irregular companies returned unsuccessful from their enterprises; and not a few turned to other sources readily at hand for accomplishment of their goals. Such an expedition entered Navajoland in December 1866.

Eighty New Mexicans, without authority either from civil or military authorities, organized a predatory band to campaign against hostile Navajos. However, after penetrating far into the interior of Indian country, and having been totally unsuccessful in their search for captives and livestock, these raiders pushed on to the Hopi village of Oraibi, where supplies could be easily obtained. Their wants satisfied, the company must have decided among themselves to attack the Puebloans, for without provocation, they assaulted the Hopis; killed three, wounded four, drove off 558 head of livestock, and carried into captivity five girls and six boys.

Once out of hostile Indian country, the New Mexicans offered their booty for sale, and profitably disposed of their captives by passing them off as Navajos. This wanton attack had come so sudden that the populace of Oraibi had been unable to resist; and as is the nature of Hopi Indians, they made no attempt to follow the New Mexicans in vengeance. Instead, they sent a delegation to Santa Fe, there to complain to the "Grand Yata," as they called the Superintendent of Indian Affairs—and "see that justice was done them."

After consulting with the Hopi delegation, the superintendent deemed the crime serious enough to warrant further attention; and Special Agent John Ward was sent out in mid-January 1867 "to investigate the matter and make a report, and if possible get possession of the captives and stock."[16] By February 10 Agent Ward had uncovered enough details of the raid to give him an idea of what lay ahead, for he wrote to Superintendent A. B. Norton, that the "task before me now is rather hard and a very disagreeable one. The captives . . . are scattered in many directions, one at Tierra Amarilla, others at Ojo Caliente, El Rito, Arroyo Seco, Taos, and some even at Los Conejos, Colorado Territory . . ."[17]

As difficult and irksome as was this task, John Ward apparently accomplished it with dispatch and efficiency. By March the Special Agent had hunted down sixty of the raiders, freed the captives, and returned fifty head of livestock. With names and facts of the case fully exposed, Superintendent Norton and his trouble-shooting agent endeavored to bring the New Mexicans to justice, by having them indicted by the grand jury during the March Session of the District Court—but their efforts failed. "The clannish nature of the Mexicans," complained Norton, "prevented their indictment. I understand that the pretext of the grand jury was that the crime (if any) was committed in the Territory of Arizona, and that they should be tried there, and not here."[18]

Although the Territory of Arizona failed to indict these slave raiders, their foray would be one of the last to penetrate Indian country. Throughout the southwest, civil and military personnel were beginning to wake up to their responsibilities. With conclusion of the Civil War national attention could once again be focused on matters other than of a military nature. Causes of turmoil between red and white men were being delved into, and a few answers uncovered as to the source of Indian hostilities—not the least of which were the nefarious practices of Indian slavery.

* * *

1. *The War of the Rebellion: A Compilation of Official Records of the Union & Confederate Armies* (Washington: 1883, Series I, Vol. IX), p. 512. Cited as *Official Records.*

2. The establishment of the Bosque Redondo Reservation was recommended by the Office of Indian Affairs on January 14, 1864, and laid before the President and approved by him on January 16, 1864. For details relative to Bosque Redondo see L. R. Bailey, *The Long Walk: A History of the Navajo Wars, 1846-68* (Los Angeles: Westernlore Press, 1964).

3. Joint Special Committee on Indian Affairs, *Condition of Tribes* (Washington: 1867), p. 336.

4. Nathan Bibo, "Reminiscences of Early Days in New Mexico," Albuquerque *Evening Herald,* June 11, 1922.

5. *Official Records,* Series I, Vol. XXVI, pp. 233-234.

6. On February 2, 1864, the commandant of Fort Wingate reported that the Navajo chief, Delgadito, had surrendered. According to official records, this Indian told "of having been attacked by a party of Mexicans, who killed some of his men, took some women and children prisoners, and drove off some of their stock . . ." Maj. E. W. Eaton To Capt. B. C. Cutler, February 2, 1864; Department of New Mexico, LR.

7. D. W. Brocheim to A.A.G., May 2, 1864; *ibid.*

8. Carson to A.A.G., April 13, 1864; *ibid.*

9. DeForrest to Edwin A. Rigg, February 19, 1864; *ibid.*

10. *Condition of Tribes,* p. 333.

11. Shaw to Cutler, May 16, 1865; Department of New Mexico, LR.

12. Shaw to Cutler, July 24, 1865; *ibid.*

13. On November 18, 1866 the U.S. Special Agent at Abiquiu agency wrote to the superintendent of Indian Affairs: "The Utes are coming here most everyday to get their powder, lead and caps; I am making the issues in small quantities as you directed me." Jesus M. Sena Baca to A. B. Norton, November 18, 1866; Superintendency Records, Letters Received from Agencies, 1866.

14. Shaw to Cutler, May 25, 1865; Department of New Mexico, LR.

15. Report to Captain Francis McCabe, July 9, 1865; *ibid.*

16. N. W. Davis to Lewis Bogy, January 18, 1867; Superintendency Papers, LR.

17. Ward to Norton, February 10, 1867; *ibid.*

18. Norton to N. G. Taylor, August 1, 1867; *ibid.*

IV

Although by 1868 Navajos had been released from their forced internment at Bosque Redondo, many of their people nevertheless remained in bondage. Hundreds of women and children still performed menial chores in households of New Mexican families. For more than twenty years Navajos had been accused of being the disruptive element to peace of the territory. They were the villains—who attacked without provocation, pilfering sheep, horses and captives from Rio Grande settlements. It was against this tribe that stringent demands were made—at times with military force —for the return of Mexican captives; and every treaty concluded with the Diné specifically insisted on the restoration of slaves.

Following the spring of 1848 campaign, and its subsequent treaty by Colonel E. W. R. Newby, Navajos willingly brought forth their captives. Again in 1849 they delivered into custody of Colonel John M. Washington, at the Pueblo of Jemez, still more Mexicans. The Meriwether Treaty of 1855, and the Bonneville

Treaty of 1858, specified delivery of captives held by the tribe, as did the Canby Treaty in 1861. The final treaty concluded between the Navajo people and the United States Government was no exception. The document, signed at Fort Sumner during summer of 1868, between tribal headmen and Peace Commissioners William T. Sherman and Colonel Samuel Tappen, likewise specified a cessation of slaving on the part of Navajos. Although these treaties outlined, in no uncertain words, mutual restoration, whereby both New Mexicans and Indians would exchange captives, the Navajos seldom benefited. For the most part, Indians carried to Rio Grande settlements and sold into slavery were lost forever to both tribe and kinsmen—and no treaty clause could induce New Mexicans to release property they had paid as high as $200 per head for.

Navajo leaders early recognized how one-sided was this issue. In January 1852, Armijo, the headman from Chuska, voiced to Agent John Greiner the feelings of his people: "My people are all crying in the same way. Three of our chiefs now sitting before you mourn for their children, who have been taken from their homes by the Mexicans. More than 200 of our children have been carried off; and we know not where they are. The Mexicans have lost but few children in comparison with what they have stolen from us . . . From the time of Colonel Newby we have been trying to get our children back. Eleven times we have given up our captives, only once have they given us ours. My people are yet crying for the children they have lost. Is it American justice that we must give up everything and receive nothing?"

John Greiner had been in the southwest long enough to know that Armijo spoke the truth. He was, however, powerless to help the Navajos. He could only promise to inform the "Great Father" of the Navajo's plight, and caution them thereafter, no more captives must be taken by either side. These words had a hollow ring, for a year-and-a-half later Zarcillas Largos complained to Navajo Agent Henry Linn Dodge about the great number of children held in captivity throughout New Mexico. As usual the issue was skirted. Both Greiner and Dodge were seasoned frontiersmen, and they knew that Indian peons were held by wealthy and influential Mexican families—who wielded the power. Any attempt to claim "their property" would likely jeopardize their public reputation, if not their very positions.

It was not until the Navajo roundup in 1863-64, that a systematic search for captives was instituted—and ensuing congressional investigations spurred the search. In the early months of 1864, General Carleton issued repeated orders for transferral of all Navajos to Bosque Redondo—be they free or slave. As was expected, New Mexicans did not readily heed the commander's dictates—they instead quietly ignored the orders. This refusal to listen to Carleton brought strong repercussions.

Garrison and post commandants throughout the territory were instructed to commence a methodical investigation to ascertain who were the holders of Navajo peons; these names to be turned over to the provost marshal's office for action and prosecution, if needs be.

The slave-trading center of Cebolleta was one of the first villages to fall under military scrutiny. In early March 1864 the commandant of Fort Wingate, Major E. W. Eaton, undertook a secret investigation. He reported, "there are at this town . . . many Indian captives, that have been taken for several years, and are now completely domesticated." Another officer, Second Lieutenant Thomas Bartlett, wrote General Carleton, "that at Altrusco there are a number of Navajo children bought from Utes; and they are in possession of the following persons: Pablo Guyago 2; Don Antonio Masco 2; Manuel Salasar 3; Lesaser Salasar 1; Antonio Vigil 1; Andreas Quintana 3; Ramon Salasar 2; Don Pablo Haremeu 2; Jose Maria Chavez 3; Juan Martinez 1—total 20."[3]

From Fort Union, military personnel searched the towns of northern New Mexico. During 1864 Second Lieutenant G. H. Arnold was the officer entrusted with this disagreeable and often dangerous task—and his reports reveal how universal was Indian bondage.

"On the 30th of August," reported Arnold, "Lt. Shout of Fort Union delivered to me one Navajo boy about 12 years old. On the 31st inst. I took possession of two women at Monton de Alamosa. On the 1st of September a woman ran away from Las Vegas and came to my camp. She says she has two children in Las Vegas and is very anxious to have them. On the 4th I took from one Taylor at Whitmore's Ranch, a Navajo girl—making five in all."[4]

Through the late summer of 1864 the army searched New Mexican settlements. Into the town of Las Vegas the investigation was carried, and a number of Navajos were released and forwarded to their reservation at Bosque Redondo. Of this group of captives, one girl in particular related, upon her release, the cruel treatment she had received—and subsequent military correspondence hints of her Mexican owner's reluctance to give her up.

"The Navajo girl, called Maria, taken by Lieutenant G. H. Arnold from Marcus Narenje, says she was captured by these people and lived with them one year and four months. That while she lived with them they treated her very badly, frequently making her take off her clothes to be whipped. She says that she was very glad to get away and does not want to go back.

"She says that the family when they saw the soldiers coming had her hide behind a table and piled bread on her and shut the door, refusing to open it when first requested to do so by the soldiers. She heard one of the Mexicans say that the soldiers would have to shoot to make them open it. The door was then opened by the family and the soldiers came in."[5]

Not all recoveries of Indian captives had such positive results, however. Often Mexican families held sec-

118

ond and third generation captives. They had lost their native language, customs and habits. No longer were they Indian; in all respects they were like their masters. To uproot these individuals was indeed a crime, and to send them to an Indian reservation was virtually exiling them to an alien land and people. Many Indian children, taken captive in infancy, had been adopted into Mexican families, baptized and brought up as Catholics. The protestations of New Mexicans against giving up such Indians were loud—and not without some degree of merit. To release these children into the hands of the military to be placed upon a reservation, would do them great injustice. These peons were Indian only in blood—they were Mexican in habit, speech and tradition.

Rosalio Colomo, a resident of Cubero, personally wrote in June 1867 to Major George W. Getty, then commanding the Department of New Mexico, begging to retain custody of an Indian child: "I have the honor to inform you that to my great regret, and that of the boy himself, on the 16th inst. an Indian boy was taken from my house. To what tribe he belongs I do not know. He was brought in by one of the campaigns against the Navajos and I have had him in my family for a short space of two years. The boy's age is not, in my opinion more than five years, and it may be easily imagined that he does not know other parents than myself and wife, nor other home than my house, which feeling he showed upon his departure. I am aware of what the law is in this regard and respect it. I did not have the boy nor did I pretend to have him in captivity other than as an adopted son, whom I have raised as such. My family have regarded him as such and he has considered himself an equal member of the family.

"You may have been informed of this by the officers at Fort Wingate by whom he was taken from my house and who witnessed the scene. It being, General, that the laws of the great Union do not extend to more than to the previous liberty of the people, which in my view is taken from this boy, he having been taken away contrary to his will from a place in which he lived contentedly and where he could enjoy the civilization to which he is entitled. I hope and ask that you will humanely return him to me if you think it is proper to do so.'"[6]

And so continued the search for Navajo women and children. Many were liberated and again reunited with their parents at Bosque Redondo. Others, as in the case of Colomo's captive boy, were deemed by military authorities, better off in the hands of their New Mexican masters—where they would grow up a part of a family; and eventually take their place in a society where integration was easily accomplished.

*　*　*

Following their release from captivity at Fort Sumner during summer of 1868, the Navajo fought their way back to economic prosperity. By tenacity of purpose, fortitude and thrift, they overcame the innumerable vicissitudes of cultural reorientation. As a people, the Navajos had been thoroughly humbled— one might say even humiliated. The Diné had suffered a defeat from which few peoples would recover. Their horses and sheep—their very subsistence and symbol of status and wealth—had been destroyed, almost to an animal. Nearly 9000 tribesmen had been forced to capitulate, and suffer the agonies of a concentration camp. As one old Navajo once voiced, "We had been beaten to the ground. Smashed to little pieces like clods. We had learned—what captivity and poverty did to our people."[7]

Their release from that desolate reservation on the Rio Pecos, however, had no effect on some Navajos, for the military, in their intensive search for Indian slaves failed to liberate many. Cleverly were these Indians concealed by their New Mexican masters. But the army had not been blind to this fact. Peace Commissioners Samuel Tappan and W. T. Sherman, upon visiting Bosque Redondo, had given way to pleadings of Navajos and granted headmen permission to carry on the search. For several years following return to red rock country. Navajos made a concerted effort to ferret out tribesmen still held in bondage. On several occasions during 1869 and 1870 Navajo chiefs—accompanied by parents of children still in captivity—visited Rio Grande settlements. Their attempts to appeal directly to the consciences of New Mexicans were entirely unsuccessful—in most cases they were not even permitted to speak to their children.

The only recourse these Indians had were to Anglo courts of law—courts of law which were established along principles having little effect upon the Mexican population, that vigorously held to the tradition of peonage. Frank Tracy Bennett, newly appointed Navajo Agent, was in full sympathy with his charges. He knew that slavery was contrary to all existing laws in the territory, as well as those of the nation. But he was, nevertheless, "convinced that any litigation would go against the Navajos, as the so-called civil authorities in all of the Mexican settlements are so prejudiced against them, that justice could not be had."

Because the military had searched for their children and had finally released the tribe—as a whole—from captivity, Navajos now looked to the United States Army for guidance in obtaining their offspring. Agent Bennett sensed this, and pleaded their cause before the Commissioner of Indian Affairs: "The Navajos believe and appreciate that their only friends are the military and other government representatives. I earnestly request, that if possible, some steps be taken to do away with this system of peonage, and have the children that are held against their will returned to their parents—as the Navajos love their children, and I think (and they claim) that they are entitled to them, the same as any race of people."[8]

As long as Mexicans held captive Navajo children there would be ill-feeling between the two peoples—

121

just as there had been during pre-Bosque Redondo days. Sensing the magnitude of the situation, the agent in January 1870 journeyed to villages lying contiguous to Navajo country, endeavoring to gain release of slaves, and hoping to iron out many of the existing difficulties between his charges and the New Mexicans. However, the "Mexicans," reported Bennett, "showed not the first sign of a disposition to settle a single case, or attempt to bring to justice any of the guilty parties. They appeared to be afraid to even give evidence or assistance of any kind."[9]

Bennett met either stern refusals to release the menials or the excuse that the children did not wish to return to their people, for they had been baptized as Catholics and reared as Mexicans. The latter may very well have been the case in a number of instances. And Bennett accepted that. The agent conceded there was little "doubt that some [captives] living with the Mexicans are better situated than they would be with their parents here. But where a question is raised and an issue made, I think they [the parents] have the same right to their children [that are under age] as any civilized people. They appear to have great love for their children, and treat them well."[10]

Through the efforts of "Big Belly," as Navajos affectionately called Frank Tracy Bennett, several children were liberated and returned to their rightful parents during 1870 and 1871. But in those cases where children voluntarily chose to remain with their New Mexican masters, there was no alternative. And to this day Navajo blood mingles with that of Mexican in the veins of the people from such towns as Abiquiu, Cebolleta, Belen and Cubero.

* * *

Agent Bennett was right when he wrote that the Navajos loved their children as much as any other people. Correspondence of the Office of Indian Affairs certain-

122

ly bears this out, for between 1872 and the early 1880s there are innumerable letters touching on the subject of Indian slavery. So too were a great many passes issued to Navajos allowing them to leave the reservation to search—on their own—the settlements of New Mexico for their offspring.

The yearnings of these people for their loved ones carried into slavery years before is indeed touching. The campaign against the tribe in 1863-1864 had unleashed their every enemy. Utes north of the Rio San Juan, the Puebloans, and New Mexicans, raided to the very heart of Navajoland—and hundreds of women and children were carried off, never to be seen or heard from again. For twenty years following that vicious campaign, Navajos never ceased in their efforts to track down their relatives and loved ones. In July 1881, Galen Eastman, Navajo Agent, granted passes to several Indians desiring to search for kin still in captivity:

Postmaster or headman,
of the town visited by the bearer:

Hosteen Soh, the bearer, headman of the Navajos is in search of his sister and a niece and stepson—aged respectively—at the time they were captured by the Utes during the Navajo was about 15 years ago then, 14—7—4 years old, add say 15—15—15 years makes them 29—22—19 years old now. These people are supposed to be [sic] sold by the Utes to the Mexicans at that time, as he has heard where some of them did reside several years ago—I informed this man, Hosteen Soh, that he must not now compel these people to return with him against their will, but if they wish to go back to their relatives then that is their right under the law and no one must hinder them. Any aid given to this man in his search for his relatives will oblige.[11]

During the next decade practically every agent was confronted by Indians seeking relatives held in slavery. On August 14, 1884, Agent John H. Bowman granted a pass of thirty days duration to a Navajo desiring to search for his daughter—taken sixteen years before "by some settlers on the Rio Grande River."[12] As late as 1886 there are still to be found in the records of the Navajo Agency, transcripts of passes permitting tribesmen to leave the reservation to seek their kin. In August of that year, prominent headman from Kin-le-chi, Ganado Mucho, and a group of his followers, were granted permission to proceed to San Rafael, New Mexico; and there "bring home, a woman, belonging to their tribe and restore her after a separation of many. years to her parents and friends."[13]

The decade of the 1880s, however, saw a change in the picture of Indian slavery—from that of Navajos searching the settlements for captives to that of an Anglo-American search for captives held by Navajos. As they had done during pre-Bosque Redondo years, wealthy tribesmen often possessed menials to help herd sheep and perform various chores around their rancherías. Carson's campaign had released most slaves held by the tribe. But many Navajos eluded the military by finding sanctuary far to the northwest, in the rugged Segi Cañon and Navajo Mountain areas.

In the summer of 1883 Navajo Agent Dennis M. Riordan began the first concerted effort to "root out" captives held by Navajos residing in the vicinity of Lukachuki. With an escort of twenty men from Fort Wingate, Riordan started from Fort Defiance on September 3, to visit a headman with a rather imposing name of Na-ki-ten-nai-be-ku-tso-he-yey, who the agent asserted, lived near the San Juan River. Five days later, Riordan, in no uncertain terms, demanded and received a number of Paiute captives from this chief.

It is rather ironic, however, that the agent had returned to his agency at Fort Defiance but a short time, before the six Paiutes for whom he had expended so much energy and time in freeing, escaped and returned to their former master. These actions no doubt bewildered the agent. Riordan's successor, John Bowman, however, offered an explanation which ethnology bears out, when he asserted that Navajo slaves were "the descendants of war captives, generations back. As according to their laws, the children always take the condition of the mother. The condition of a slave here, does not seem so very hard, because there is not a very strong contract between masters and slaves."[14]

The Bureau of Indian Affairs, with its usual lack of tact and understanding, demanded the release of all slaves held by the tribe. Manuelito, Chief of the eastern Navajos, was one of the first headmen to be approached. Reputed to have several slaves, he was ordered by Bowman to release them to Anglo custody. Agent John Bowman soon found out, as had Riordan, that many captives were reluctant to leave their masters. When the agent demanded release of Manuelito's slaves, the old warrior quietly remarked "that he did not claim control over them in any way, that they were perfectly at liberty to go anywhere or do anything they wished; that he considered them all as members of his family, not as slaves." In fact at that very meeting, Manuelito was accompanied by one of his "slaves" who, reported the agent, was married "to a woman who is also a slave of Manuelito's, and they have several children." When given the choice of remaining with the old war chief or taking up residence at Fort Defiance and placing their children in the boarding school recently constructed there, the slave replied that he would rather remain in "captivity."

Agent Bowman, in his report to the Commissioner of Indian Affairs, summed up the situation of Navajo slaves with these wise comments: "These people do not seem to be controlled altogether by fear of their masters; they seem inclined to, 'bear those ills they have, than fly to others that they know not of.' The question of slavery among these Indians is a peculiar one to deal with. Ignorance and custom has forged chains for them too strong to be easily broken—they are not capable of any other condition, do not want to be liberated, and I cannot see how we are to do it. It is like guarding a jail to keep criminals from breaking in."[15]

Agent John Bowman never wrote truer words, for times had changed considerably. Forty years before, slave trading had been a lucrative business, with all western tribes participating in it. At times the relationships in that nefarious commerce seemed, and indeed was, rather vague: Utes raided Paiutes, Navajos raided Paiutes, Utes raided Navajos, Navajos raided Utes, Apaches raided Navajos—and Mexicans raided them all. With the final breaking of Navajo resistance by the Carleton-Carson campaign, the tribe's participation in the slave trade ceased altogether. The few slaves which remained in their custody had, as Bowman stated, been taken long before, and had escaped the Navajo round-up. It was true, many were descendants of captives, and knew no other existence than servitude, but it was impossible to separate these individuals from their masters. Many had the same rights as other tribal members—especially women, who often became wives to Navajo bucks. Male captives, however, had a somewhat difficult status. Their integration was not accomplished so easily. As Bowman stated, the Navajo being a matrilinear people, traced descent through the female side. Thus male captives remained in a servile position, although they could take wives, usually other captive females. As Riordan had discovered, these slaves wanted none of the Anglo-American version of liberation. Those who were freed, went quickly back to their masters. And to this day, their descendants are with the tribe—although certainly not in the same status, for they are Navajo in appearance and tradition.

*   *   *

1. Abel, *Calhoun Correspondence,* p. 467.

2. Maj. E. W. Eaton to Capt. B. C. Cutler, March 3, 1864; Department of New Mexico, LR.

3. Bartlett to Carleton, April 1, 1865; *ibid.*

4. Arnold to Capt. H. B. Bristol, Sept. 6, 1864; *ibid.*

5. Statement of Brig. General M. M. Crocker, Nov. 2, 1864; *ibid.*

6. Colomo to Getty, June 23, 1867; *ibid.*

7. Ethnographic notes, Richard Van Valkenburg Collection, in the Arizona Pioneers' Historical Society, Tucson.

8. Bennett to Clinton, August 19, 1870; Records of the New Mexico Superintendency, LR.

9. *Ibid.*

10. Bennett to William Clinton, Feb. 1, 1870; *Ibid.,* Letter Received from Agencies.

11. Fort Defiance Letter Book, September 12, 1880 to September 10, 1881, Letter No. 383, dated July 28, 1881. A microfilm copy of these press-books is in the archives of the Arizona Pioneers' Historical Society.

12. Pass (dated August 14, 1884), and letter No. 227; in *ibid.,* June 27 to Sept. 27, 1884.

13. Pass granted by S. S. Patterson (dated Aug. 1, 1886) in *ibid.,* July 1, 1886 to Jan. 10, 1887; also letter No. 69.

14. Bowman to Commissioner, Aug. 1, 1884; *ibid.,* June 27 to Sept. 27, 1884, Letter No. 160.

15. Bowman to Commissioner (n.d.), in *ibid.,* May 15, 1884 to April 1, 1885, letter No. 92.

SECTION THREE

Slave Raiders In The Great Basin 1760-1855

I

That vast inland sink, extending from the eastern slopes of the Sierra Nevada Mountains of California to the western flanks of the Wasatch Mountains of Utah, and from southeast Oregon and Idaho to southern Nevada, was labeled by "Pathfinder" John C. Fremont— the Great Basin. And appropriately named it was, for it is an area of nearly 200,000 square miles having no outlet to the sea. For the most part it is an arid, inhospitable land of bleached desert playas, seemingly endless salt flats, rugged mountain ranges, and shriveled water courses. In short, an area which indelibly left its mark upon native peoples dwelling within its confines.[1]

Most, if not all Indians inhabiting this vast region were related linguistically—speaking various dialects of Shoshonean. The sparsity of subsistence is reflected in the meagerness of their culture's content, and in their simple social structure. Problems of daily existence restricted large tribal groupings with complex socioeconomic patterns. Instead, these Indians, known as Paiutes, ranged the Great Basin in aggregates no larger than extended families, scratching out a precarious livelihood. It was because of their seemingly low culture, that Paiutes were held in disgust and regarded as little more than animals by not only white men, but by other tribes as well. In 1830 chroniclers for a party of Anglo-American trappers, led by William Wolfskill, aptly expressed current sentiments regarding "Digger Indians"—as these people would contemptuously be called at a later date:

> These people are an anomaly—apparently the lowest species of humanity, approaching the monkey. Nothing but their straight form entitles them to the name of man. They had not a hatchet, or any instruments to cut or perforate the softest wood. One discovery they had made, or had learned . . . from the more intelligent savage— they would get fire by rubbing pieces of hardwood, but it was a long and tedious process. They have but few words and communicate chiefly by signs. They live in little clans scattered over a great extent of country . . . Their food consists of occasionally a rabbit, with roots and mice, grasshoppers and insects such as flies, spiders and worms of every kind. Where nuts exist, they gather them for food. They also luxuriate and grow fat when they find a patch of clover. On many kinds of grass, they feed like cattle. They love to be covered with lice because they appropriate these for food.[2]

It would seem, therefore, that the bleak environment of the Great Basin, with its impoverished inhabitants offered little to attract that wandering merchant—the Indian trader. In the strict sense of the word this was true. There were few beaver and no buffalo in this land; and even if there were, Paiutes were too preoccupied in scratching their meager existence from the earth to trap or hunt these items of barter. Regardless, these abject people would feel the commerce of the Indian trader—and feel it hard.

* * *

The eastern limits of the Great Basin are brought to an abrupt halt by the Wasatch Mountains, Utah's rugged backbone. This range, and the lands eastward as far as the Rocky Mountains and the area southeastward to the Spanish settlements along the upper Rio Grande of New Mexico, was the domain of the Utes. These people were more fortunate than their cousins, the Paiutes, for they were in line of direct contact with the Spanish settlements; and later Spanish exploration and expansion northward and westward—and were destined to produce the one essential which would change their socio-economic patterns, raising them to the status of foremost intermediaries in the Spanish-Indian trade, and make them the scourge of the lowly Paiutes.

With approach of Spanish traders during the latter decades of the 18th century, the Utes were quick to grasp the economic gains at hand. Acquisition of the horse increased Ute mobility and altered his social structure. Bands formerly having little political coherence now united under war leaders, who owed their power to their ability to keep their followers mounted. And these petty headmen would eventually go far afield to accomplish their aims. Timpanogos Utes from the Utah Lake region raided as far as southern California for blooded Spanish stock. Capote Utes forded the Rio San Juan to obtain livestock from Navajos; and eastern Ute bands sent forays onto the Central Plains to raid the Comanche, Plains Apache and Pawnee. The majority of Ute livestock, however, came directly from New Mexican settlements—and the animals were bartered, not pilfered. At first tanned buckskin, furs, and dried buffalo meat constituted the mediums of exchange demanded by the Spanish. Not many years would pass before other wares would be sought in the Indian trade—captives.

By the early 1760s tribes between the Wasatch and Rocky Mountains were being well exploited by New Mexican traders from Taos and Abiquiu. Although records of their junkets are meager, a few brief accounts of trading expeditions still survive, which give some indication of the intensity of the commerce at that time. In 1765, a Juan María de Rivera left Santa Fe, proceeded northward to the Rio San Juan; and skirted the northern spurs of the La Plata Mountains of present-day Colorado, to reach the Dolores River. Rivera then swung eastward, crossing the great Uncompahgre Plateau, and followed the river of the same name to the Rio Gunnison, where he halted to trade with Utes of that region.

The following decade saw other merchants from the Rio Grande penetrate the wilderness to the north and west to trade with Utes. Pedro Mora, Gregorio Sandoval, Andrés Muniz, and many more ventured north; and by 1775 men of like caliber were spending "two, three, and four months at a time" trading with Utes. However, it was not until 1776 that interest was really stimulated in the area to the immediate west—the Great Basin.

In July of that year two Franciscan friars, Silvestra Velez de Escalante and Francisco Atanasio Dominguez, with an escort of eight men, left Santa Fe, determined to locate a feasible route to Monterey, California. This party proceeded northwest to present-day Utah Lake, where they spent three days near what is today the town of Provo. Journeying south to the Sevier Valley, the friars encountered increasingly rough terrain and were eventually deserted by their guides. Thus forced to abandon their plans for the overland trip to California, the party returned to Santa Fe, by way of a southern route through the Hopi villages.[4] Although a failure, Escalante's expedition opened the Great Basin to New Mexican traders; and for several years thereafter commerce waxed strong. By the 1790s most Utes residing in the Uintah Basin and along the fertile western piedmont of the Wasatch—Utah Lake and the Sevier Valley—were mounted on New Mexican horses.

As with all trading relationships, however, difficulties began looming on the horizon; grave enough, in this case, to disturb the economic equilibrium. Spanish officials were becoming concerned over the fact that unscrupulous traders were placing into Ute hands large quantities of weapons; and that unjust dealings might occasion trouble with mountain tribes. As a result a *bando* was issued on September 13, 1778, seeking to control the flow of contraband goods to border tribes, by prohibiting trade by "unlicensed traders."[5] The *bando* of 1778, however, was ineffectual, and unlicensed traders continued to visit Utes, as well as the Paiutes of the Great Basin.

Despite illegal trade activities, peace and a close relationship existed between the Spanish and Utes from Escalante's time until 1805. In that year correspondence of the Governor of New Mexico, Joaquin de Real Alencaster, hinted of possible breakdown of relations. In a letter to his commandant-general (dated September 1), the governor praised an old *genizaro* (mestizo), Manuel Mestas, for "pacifying the Utes" about Lake Timpanogos (Utah Lake), and recovering Spanish livestock.[6]

Spanish officials had every right to be concerned about their dealings with neighboring tribes, for the commerce had taken a far more sinister turn. No longer were peltries and jerked buffalo meat the mediums of exchange with the Utes. The very founding of Spanish colonies in the New World had been based upon slave labor—and the province of New Mexico was no exception. Wealthy householders and *rancheros* along the Rio Grande Valley were in need of menials and *pastores*—and the Indian trade offered solution to the labor shortage. Women and children snatched from roving bands of the Great Basin were tractable and made excellent servants. Paiute groups such as Shivwits, Piedes, Uinkarets, and Gosiutes now became the objectives of lightning-fast raids of the Utes.

By 1812 the slave trade had reached such proportion that Utes were well mounted, and even better armed than New Mexicans. Added to this, flaring of tribal warfare was the inevitable result of slave raiding—much to the consternation of Spanish lawmakers. In that year another *bando* was passed attempting to regulate the Indian trade by prohibiting the purchase of captives from the Utes. But the roots of the Indian trade had penetrated too deeply—and this insidious commerce could not be halted by mere passage of legislation. The illegal traffic with the Utes continued for the next fifty years, with horses, guns, and slaves being the chief items of barter.[7]

History of the trade in human flesh, however, is exceedingly difficult to reconstruct. In years following 1812, the trade was clandestine; and for the most part those Spaniards participating in it were illiterate, and government officials were either blind to its effects, or merely turned their heads the other way. The only records available until advent of the meticulous Mormon chroniclers in mid-1800s, are those of court proceedings—and those are few indeed.

One report of a legal proceeding, held in 1813, is indicative of the spread of the slave traffic. An expedition of seven men, under leadership of Maurico Arze and Largos García, left the frontier settlement of Abiquiu on the Rio Chama on March 16, to trade with Utes. Upon the party's return, five months later, they were immediately apprehended and brought before Manuel García, Alcalde of the Villa de Santa Cruz de la Cañada, for failing to have proper trade credentials, as well as having twelve Indian captives in their possession. The notarized accounts of the hearing relate that the Arze-García expedition had proceeded to Utah Valley, where they remained three days waiting

136

for the Indians to assemble, so that trade could commence. When the Utes finally gathered, according to Arze and García, the Indians would barter nothing but Paiute slaves—"as they had done on other occasions." When this offer was rejected, the Indians became infuriated, and before their chiefs succeeded in quieting the tribesmen, eight horses and one mule belonging to the Spaniards had been killed.

Collecting their remaining animals, the Spanish traders departed the next morning for the Sanpete Valley and the Rio Colorado beyond. It was while upon the latter stream that García-Arze encountered the Ute chief after which Utah's principal mountains are named —Chief Wasatch. At first the traders were greeted cordially by the Indian and his followers, but when slaves were offered, the Spaniards again refused to barter, and hostilities threatened anew. Deciding to prevent possible injury to themselves, the traders agreed to take twelve slaves and 109 pelts in exchange for their horses. The bargain consummated, the Spaniards headed homeward.[8]

If the Arze-García case can be taken as any indication of the extent of the slave traffic, it is certainly obvious that the commerce had spread by 1813 throughout the length and breadth of what is today the state of Utah; and was being carried on by some of the most illustrious Indian leaders. The desire openly expressed by Utes to trade only slaves, is further evidence of the tremendous profits which must have existed in the traffic. And traders were certainly penetrating Ute country in large enough numbers to instill a desire for trade only in this human commodity.

*   *   *

For the next two decades the spread of the slave trade was rapid, extending from what is today Colorado through Utah and Nevada to California. The Old Spanish Trail, blazed in part by Friar Escalante, now became the main artery over which flowed the human commodity. By 1830 this trail, commencing at Abiquiu, had become the established route between New Mexico and Los Angeles—by way of the Great Basin. Entering Utah near the present town of Moab, it snaked its way through Emery County, passed over the Wasatch Mountains, traversed Salina Cañon to the Sevier Valley. It then proceeded southward through Marysvale Cañon to the present town of Spry, where it diverted westward to Cedar City, passing through the infamous Mountain Meadows to the Santa Clara River. From that point in extreme southwestern Utah, the Old Spanish Trail continued to Las Vegas, Nevada, thence to southern California and the Pueblo of Los Angeles.[9]

The mild climate of southern California with its ample rainfall produced pasturage for immense herds of horses and cattle, which became the commodities of overland trade; and in many cases were exchanged for women and children, carried over tortuous miles, bound to backs of mules.[10] So systematic was conduct of the California-New Mexican slave trade that it resulted in tremendous profits to its participants. Seasonal trading ventures were fitted out in Santa Fe, Taos and Abiquiu. The first stop on the trader's itinerary would be with Utes or Navajos, with whom guns and trinkets were exchanged for horses. These animals were then sorted according to grades by the New Mexicans —the poorer mounts being reserved for exchange with "Digger" Paiutes, who would often relinquish their children for a fat mule or a horse to eat. The traders would then continue to California, where the Paiute children were bartered for still more horses, or sold outright for cash. On the return trip, this process would be repeated—the women and children being taken back to New Mexico and sold as menials—at the current rate of $100 for a boy, and from $150 to $200 for healthy girls, who were in greater demand as house servants.[11]

New Mexican caravans traveling to-and-fro along

the Old Spanish Trail were well organized, and often strung out for miles along the route. G. Douglas Brewerton, returning to New Mexico in 1846 with Christopher "Kit" Carson, had ample opportunity to observe and vividly describe these traders in one of the leading journals of his day:

> This caravan consists of some two or three hundred Mexican traders who go on one year to . . . California . . . with a supply of blankets and other articles of New Mexican manufacture; and having disposed of their goods, invest . . . in California mules and horses, which they drive back across the desert.

Brewerton was fascinated by these traders and he meticulously noted every detail, even as to the shape of buttons on the clothes worn by the motley crews:

> Their appearance was grotesque . . . Imagine upward of two hundred Mexicans dressed in every variety of costume, from the embroidered jacket of the wealthy Californian, with its silver bell-shaped buttons, to the scanty habiliments of the skin-clad Indians.[12]

Although there were some individuals in California who welcomed the insidious slave trade, others openly protested that the traffic violated human rights, and only led to hostilities with Indian tribes. On July 13, 1824, the California provincial governor passed a decree forbidding the Indian slave trade. Again, court cases reflect the fact that the now clandestine commerce could not be halted by mere passage of laws.

In 1833 California officials investigated a case involving the sale of an Indian youth. One José Roche was apprehended trying to conclude a purchase of an Indian from a New Mexican trader, Juan Sanchez, for the sum of $70. In his defense, Roche pleaded that he had purchased the boy with intentions of adopting and raising him according to the principles of Catholicism—the Indian being released from bondage on attainment of legal age. Still another case, in January of that same year, sheds further light on the fact that the slave trade was very much alive. On January 8 a Californian, Ignacio del Valle, reported to the alcalde of Los Angeles, that a New Mexican named Francisco Vigil, had tried to sell him an Indian boy. Valle, however, declined the offer for fear of prosecution; and the trader apparently returned to New Mexico before he could be apprehended.[13]

Fact that the Indian slave traffic was on the increase after 1830—despite legislation in both New Mexico and California—was highlighted by Anglo-American mountain man, "Uncle" Dick Wootton. This grizzled old frontiersman, while trapping in the Wasatch Mountains from 1837 to 1838, frequently came upon New Mexican slave trading expeditions, of whom he states:

> (it) was no uncommon thing in those days to see a party of Mexicans in that country buying Indians. And while we were trapping there, I sent a lot of peltries to Taos by a party of those same slave traders.[14]

The period from 1830 to mid-1840s was the height of the Great Basin slave trade. Age and sex of Indian captives seemed to have been the prime factors in all transactions. The tractable nature, willingness and efficiency of Paiutes, were the next considerations in weighing the value of captives. The price of Paiutes, at the time, was not too exorbitant. Thomas J. Farnham related in 1839 that "the price of these slaves in the market of New Mexico varies with age and other qualities of the person. Those from ten to fifteen years sell from $50 to $100, which is by no means an extravagant price, when we take into consideration the herculean task of cleansing them fit for the market."

* * *

The weakness of Shoshonean social culture, together with the influx of horses and other trade commodities, produced additional factors contributing to rise of the slave trade. These Indians were split into numerous bands, with no overall political unity, offering a ripe opportunity for a man with a little influence to gather together a few lodges and create a new band.[15] Such a person, destined to become one of the foremost traffickers of slaves, arose among the Utes. Walkara,[16] son of a clan chieftain, was born in a Timpanogas Ute village on the Spanish Fork River about 1808. Tribal warfare, however, broke up his father's clan early in Walkara's childhood, and he spent most of his early years among the Paiutes of Utah Valley.

If ever there was an Indian that typified the qualities of leadership desired by Utes, Walkara possessed or soon developed them all. He was "of imposing appearance," standing over six feet in height; and his hawk-like facial features and penetrating eyes soon gave him the name—"Hawk-of-the-Mountains." As Walkara reached manhood he traveled extensively through the tribes of the Great Basin and mingled freely with Mexican traders. He became well-versed in several Indian dialects, spoke Spanish fluently; and through his acquaintance with Anglo-American mountain men gained a working knowledge of English. A crack shot with both rifle and pistol, Walkara was any man's match in physical combat. He was inured to fatigue and could stay in the saddle for days at a time. In diplomacy he was subtle, and possessed powers as an orator. And in the manner of Utes, Walkara was vain and cruel.[17]

Walkara's commanding physique and qualities of leadership drew to him other young renegades; and around his four brothers, Arrapeen, Sanpitch (San Pete), Ammon, and Tobiah (Tabby), Walkara shaped his band. It was composed of the best men from

Paiutes, Utes, Snakes, and at times, even such white adventurers as Pegleg Smith and the mulatto mountain man, James Beckwourth—and it was the latter man, who gave Walkara's "richly caparisoned" cavalry the name—*chaquetones*.[18]

Like other Utes, Walkara regarded the horse as his most important single possession[19]—but his desire did not stop there. To him the horse was an all-important essential in his climb upwards as a war-chief; and Walkara very early in life became possessed with the desire for horses with which to mount his warriors, and carry on trade with Mexicans, Anglo-Americans, and the surrounding tribes. By mid-1830s, this Ute was raiding neighboring tribes, but his lust was boundless and he soon turned far afield for mounts. By 1840 residents of the San Bernardino Valley of Southern California, were bitterly complaining that "the moon has come again and with it the dread Py-Utahs." Across the Rio Colorado, over the Mojave Desert and through Cajon Pass, rode Walkara and his warriors. Mission herds and prized *rancho* stock fell to this Ute's swift raids—never in the history of the West had there emerged a greater horse thief.[20]

Walkara was also quick to learn the eagerness of the Mexicans to procure menials for their homes and fields. For a woman or a healthy youngster, New Mexicans would trade one horse. If delivered to Santa Fe, Taos or Abiquiu, the slave would bring double in horses or silver. Between 1832 and 1835—perhaps even before he won the title of "greatest horse thief in history"—Walkara had established himself as lord of the Mexican-Indian slave traffic in the interior basin. Up and down the Old Spanish Trail, from the Wasatch Mountains to the Sierras, and from the country of the Snakes to that of the Navajos, Walkara and his *chaquetones,* made themselves felt. They levied a taxation of blankets and buckskin, as well as for fighting men, upon the southern Paiutes. Often these "digger" bands

142

were unable to meet the stringent demands, and in lieu of this the Ute chief took their children.[21]

The various Paiute bands were at the mercy of Walkara's slave raiders; and distinctly felt the disadvantage of not being mounted. By early 1840s, Walkara and his *chaquetones* were fearfully spoken of in every village between the Sierra Nevada Mountains and the Rockies. Not only did those Indians furnishing women and children fear him, but his own tribesmen, and even the New Mexicans, were reluctant to cross the Ute chief when he demanded tribute, or a woman to sleep with when in their settlements.[22] Walkara had indeed risen a long way—from a son of a minor clan chief to the "greatest horse thief in history" and the principal supplier of Indian slaves.

However, in the years prior to 1850 Walkara would experience developments which would gradually lift from his hands the control of the slave traffic, and eventually halt it altogether. By the late 1830s New Mexicans, seeking to eliminate the middleman in the trade, were themselves raiding Indian villages; and in 1846-1847, Walkara's scouts brought word of long wagon trains of "Mormonees" rolling westward toward the Ute realm. To this Indian, these people may have heralded the hope of a new field in which to ply his trade in horses and slaves. But to Walkara's surprise, he would soon find the Mormons a far different breed than the Mexicans, for they, according to the doctrine of their faith, sought not to enslave the Indians but to make them again a "delightful people."

* * *

1. For a geographical and historical discussion of the Great Basin see: Gloria G. Cline, *Exploring the Great Basin* (Norman: University of Oklahoma Press, 1963).

2. J. Cecil Alter (ed.), "Journal of Orange Clark & George Yount," *California Historical Quarterly* (Vol. II, April, 1923), p. 13.

3. For an excellent discussion of the influence of the horse upon Ute culture consult: Gottfried O. Lang, *The White Rock Utes in Transition* (Salt Lake: University of Utah Press).

4. A detailed account of Escalante's penetration of the Great Basin is found in: Herbert E. Bolton, *Pageant in the Wilderness; the Story of the Escalante Expedition to the Interior Basin, 1776* (Salt Lake: Utah Historical Society, 1950).

5. This *bando* is listed as No. 740 in R. E. Twitchell, *The Spanish Archives of New Mexico* (Cedar Rapids: Torch Press, 1914), Vol. II, p. 263. The original document is preserved in the archives of the Museum of New Mexico, Santa Fe.

6. William J. Snow, "Utah Indian & Spanish Slave Trade," *Utah Historical Quarterly* (Vol. II, July 1929), p. 68.

7. A brief discussion of slave raiding in the Great Basin is offered by Mormon historians LeRoy and Ann Hafen, *The Old Spanish Trail* (Glendale: Arthur H. Clark, 1954), pp. 263-264.

8. Documents relating to the Arze-García case are listed in Twitchell, *op. cit.*, p. 577, No. 2511 See also Leland H. Creer, "Spanish American Slave Trade in the Great Basin, 1800-1853," *New Mexico Historical Review* (Vol. XXIX, July 1941), pp. 175-176; and Snow, *op. cit.*, pp. 68-69.

9. Creer, *ibid.*, pp. 176-177.

10. LeRoy & Ann Hafen, *op. cit.*, p.269.

11. This account of the California-New Mexico slave traffic is given by Mormon missionary and frontiersman, Daniel W. Jones, in a recently republished book: *Forty Years Among the Indians* (Los Angeles: Westernlore Press, 1960), pp. 47-48.

12. G. Douglas Brewerton, "A Ride with Kit Carson," *Harper's New Monthly Magazine* (Vol. VIII, April 1854), pp. 312-313.

13. Hafen, *op. cit.*, pp. 169-270.

14. H. L. Conrad, *Uncle Dick Wootton: Pioneer Frontiersman* (Chicago 1890), pp. 75-76.

15. Edward Palmer, *Notes on the Utah Utes, 1866-1877*, edited by Robert F. Heizer (Salt Lake: University of Utah Press, 1954), p. 4.

16. Early day observer of Indian ways, William R. Palmer, claimed that Walkara derived his name from the Ute word "Wahker" (yellow). "The Indians named their babies for anything that attracted attention or interest and for such reason, this baby was called yellow." This was later anglicized into Walker. Palmer, "Pahute Indian Government and Law," *Utah Historical Quarterly* (Vol. II, April 1929), p. 37.

17. For biological data on the Ute see Paul Bailey, *Walkara, Hawk of the Mountains* (Los Angeles: Westernlore Press, 1954).

18. *Chaqueta*, a short jacket of the type worn by mountain men. *Ibid.*, p. 14.

19. Lang, *Loc. cit.*, p. 8.

20. Father Juan Caballeria, *History of San Bernardino Valley* (San Bernardino, 1902), p. 103.

21. Palmer, "Pahute Government," *op. cit.*, p. 40.

22. Bailey, *op. cit.*, p. 14.

II

The Mormons, entering Salt Lake Valley in 1847, came face-to-face with the turmoil caused by the Indian slave traffic. Their chroniclers wrote of problems presented by this trade—and for the first time, a clear picture of the commerce emerges. Diaries of missionaries; the writings of Mormon leader, Brigham Young; headlines in the *Deseret News,* and the meticulously kept *Journal History* of the Church of Jesus Christ of Latter-day Saints—all reveal amazing insights into the character of the tribe.

*   *   *

Walkara first saw the Mormon settlement of the arid Salt Lake Valley, not as an encroachment upon his lands but as a golden opportunity to enrich himself and his band; and the "Hawk" wasted little time in contacting the Mormons and bidding them welcome. He freely consented to letting the Saints sink their plows into Ute soil and never objected to sharing his fisheries at Utah Lake. In fact, Walkara begged Brigham Young to send his people southward to occupy lands and establish trade with Utes along the Sevier and Virgin Rivers—lands over which Walkara held sway. Had it not been for this Ute's hand of welcome—no matter what the motive—Mormons would never have peacefully founded their "Zion" in the Great Basin. As it was, a year later the Great Salt Lake Valley had a population of nearly 2,000 Saints, who had constructed 450 buildings, three sawmills, one temporary flour mill, and had broken ground for miles upon miles of irrigation canals.

Walkara was truly amazed at the industry of these hardy people; and felt that surely they would welcome Ute trade—and perhaps would even desire menials to labor in their fields, as had the New Mexicans. During the winter of 1847-48; Arrapeen, brother of Walkara, rode to the Hot Springs north of Salt Lake City. With a group of braves, together with several Paiute children, Arrapeen's hopes were high for a successful trading venture.[1]

Upon arrival at the Hot Springs, Arrapeen offered the children to the Saints in trade for horses and arms. To the Indian's amazement, these people seemed horrified by his offer, and they refused to trade for the children at any price. Indignant at the Mormons' rebuff, Arrapeen tersely replied, "that the children were captured in the war and would be killed at sunset if the whites did not buy them." The Mormons thereupon purchased a young girl, and the other was shot, as the Indian had promised.[2]

The Utes now realized that the Mormons could be intimidated into purchasing Indian captives; and the Saints were approached on every occasion. In 1851 Walkara personally paid the recently established Mormon farming community of Parowan a visit. With the Ute chief and his *chaquetones* were three Paiute children. During the Indians' brief visit these children were tied to a sagebrush to grub about the ground for edible seeds and grass which, according to one observer, "they did with good relish." Again the Mormons were struck with pity, and the captives were released upon the trade of three horses.[3]

Not only were Utes plaguing the Mormons, but New Mexican slave-raiders and procurers were streaming into Utah by scores. Regular rendezvous were being held about the shores of Utah Lake and at points along the Sevier River, at which the Utes would exchange their captives for horses, guns and ammunition packed from the New Mexican communities of Abiquiu, Taos and Santa Fe.

So brisk was this trade that New Mexican communities on the upper Rio Grande owed their very existence to this commerce with the Utes; and their governing officials were issuing licenses to trade with the Indians with no mention as to the items of barter.[4] Even the Superintendent of Indian Affairs for the Territory of New Mexico and his employees aided and abetted the slave trade in Utah—although perhaps unwittingly. As the Utes were considered as being at peace with the Anglo-Americans, officials of the Office of Indian Affairs saw no wrong in granting licenses to trade with these people. The only requirement of a person seeking such a permit, was specification of the number of animals and packs being taken into Indian country—and the promise that he would not trade guns, ammunition and whiskey. Never once was the question of trading women and children brought up, although this aspect of the commerce was well known at the time.[5]

By 1851 Mormon leader, Brigham Young, was aroused by this situation, and decided to end slavery once and for all in the area under his jurisdiction. As Governor and newly appointed Superintendent of Indian Affairs for the Territory of Utah, he vowed to halt the insidious traffic through the powers vested in him by the Government of the United States. The Governor sought out New Mexican traders operating in his jurisdiction, explained to them that the war with Mexico and the subsequent Treaty of Guadalupe de Hidalgo

149

had placed the territory under United States control and that all traders were obligated to observe the laws of that country. Brigham further reprimanded the traders, by informing them that the traffic in human beings was a cruel practice, causing war and bloodshed among Great Basin tribes. Despite most promises given by New Mexican traders not to operate in Utah, there were still a few who persisted in daring the wrath of the Mormon "lion."

In the fall of 1851, three parties of New Mexican slave procurers were at work in Utah, one of which was apprehended in San Pete County, shortly after they entered the territory. Armed with a trade license signed by James S. Calhoun, Superintendent of Indian Affairs for New Mexico, this group under leadership of a Pedro León, made known their desire to trade horses for Indian children.

Learning of León's activities, Mormon officials acted fast. Arrested and brought before Judge Zerubbabel Snow of the First District Court at Salt Lake City, León and associates pleaded their case. The Paiutes, according to their defense, had stolen eighteen of their animals. The traders applied, and were granted Mormon approval to pursue and reclaim their livestock. Trailing the Indians, the New Mexicans found their animals had been devoured by the hungry Paiutes, and the only remuneration that the Indians offered León and his men were nine children (four girls and five boys), which were "reluctantly" accepted in lieu of the horses. Despite this defense, the traders were found guilty, fined $50 each; and expelled "on foot" from the Territory of Utah.[6]

This flagrant disregard of Mormon authority by León and other traders from New Mexico greatly aroused the Saints to action; and on November 15, 1851, the *Deseret News* issued fair warning to all who might venture into Utah seeking Indian slaves:

The purchase and removal of Indian children

from Utah territory to any other state or territory, or the removal of Indian children without purchase to any other territory by such means or processes as appears to have been contemplated by said men [León, *et al*], is kidnapping in the eyes of the United States law and ought to be treated so in any United States court.

Not only were León and his party badly treated by Mormons seeking to halt the slave traffic, but other New Mexicans suffered as well from the iron will of Brigham Young. In mid-July 1853, Edward F. Beale, the newly appointed Superintendent of Indian Affairs for California, met a party of New Mexicans fleeing out of Utah. The chronicler of Beale's overland trip to California, Gwinn Harris Heap, wrote that "these men reported that they had been badly treated by the Mormons at the Vegas de Santa Clara; and that two of their number had been put in jail. They warned us to be on our guard, when we arrived in Utah Territory, as they (the Mormons) had threatened to shoot or imprison all Americans passing through their country." Heap, however, correctly passed this advice off with this casual remark: "Not withstanding their plausible story, the Mexicans only impressed us with the belief that, having misbehaved, they had received the chastisement they deserved, for it was well known to us that the Mormons strictly prohibited the practice of natives of New Mexico of bartering firearms and ammunition with the Indians for their children."

Although the León episode and subsequent expulsion of others from Utah, convinced New Mexicans of the dangers involved in plying their trade in lands under Mormon jurisdiction, it only served to infuriate the Utes. With tightening of Mormon control came the necessity of moving trading rendezvous—which greatly displeased these Indians. Now Walkara and other Ute chieftains were forced to cross the Rio San Juan or the Colorado River to Navajoland to trade Paiute women and children with intermediaries there; no venture into New Mexican settlements, which was always a hazardous enterprise. However, the hope was not dead within Walkara that Mormons would finally consent to the slave trade.

In 1852 Arrapeen encamped in the foothills above Provo, and once again offered children to the Saints. When Arrapeen received a blunt refusal, he became enraged and stated that "the Mormons had stopped the Mexicans from buying these children; they had no right to do so unless they bought them themselves." Then resorting to the only method he knew to clinch the argument, the Ute, "took one of these children by the heels and dashed it on the hard ground," after which he threw the body toward the Mormons, telling them as he did so, that "they had no hearts or they would have bought the child and saved its life."

The Mormon leaders were not hard-hearted men. The virtual overrunning of Utah Territory by slave procurers, and the now belligerent actions of Ute headmen, fully impressed the Mormons of the inevitable fate awaiting other captives. On January 5, 1852, Brigham Young presented to the Utah Legislature his unique proposal for halting Indian slavery—"by purchasing the Indian into freedom."

The practice of purchasing Indian children for slaves is a trade carried on by the Mexican population of New Mexico and California. These traders of late years have extended their traffic into the limits of this territory. This trade I have endeavored to prevent, and this fall, happening to encounter a few of them in my travels, as superintendent of Indian affairs, strictly prohibited their further traffic. The majority of them appeared satisfied and after making a few exchanges of property in the settlements, returned to their own country; unfortunately, however, a few of them still determined to carry on their nefarious traffic;

they have been arrested, and are now on their trial in this city.

It is unnecessary perhaps for me to indicate the true policy for Utah in regard to slavery. Restrictions of law and government make all servants, but human flesh to be dealt in as property, is not consistent or compatible with the true principles of government [sic]. My own feelings are, that no property can or should be recognized as existing in slaves either Indian or African. No person can purchase them without their becoming as free, so far as natural rights are concerned, as persons of any color; under the present low and degraded situation of the Indian race, so long as the practice of gambling away, selling or otherwise disposing of their children; as also sacrificing prisoners obtained among them, it seems indeed that any transfer would be to them a relief and a benefit. Many a life by this means is saved; many a child redeemed from the thraldom of savage barbarity, and placed upon equal footing with the more favored portions of the human race. If in return for favors and expense which may have been incurred on their account, services should be considered due, it would become necessary that some law should provide the suitable regulations under which all such indebtedness be defrayed.

This may be said to present a new feature in the traffic of human beings; it is essentially purchasing them into freedom, instead of slavery, but it is not the low servile drudgery of Mexican slavery, to which I would doom them, not to be raised among beings scarcely superior to themselves, but where they could find that consideration pertaining not only to civilized, but humane and benevolent society. . . .[9]

The Territorial Legislature sensed the wisdom in this unusual plan, and concurred wholeheartedly with

Brigham. It would, indeed, be far better to place these Indian children in Latter Day Saint homes, where they would receive love and education, than subject them to the inhuman treatment of New Mexican slave procurers. Therefore, with an earnest desire to end Indian slavery and raise the status of subjected Indians, the Territorial Legislature on March 7, 1852, passed and approved the necessary laws for the relief of Indians held in Captivity.[10]

Events during 1853 convinced Governor Young that his enacted legislation was not enough to curb the illegal and clandestine trade. Reports were received almost weekly of New Mexican traders operating within Utah Territory; and the number of guns in possession of the Utes worried Mormon officials. In fact, the slave trade was a menace to Mormon missionary endeavors among the various tribes. In one such report from William M. Wall (dated May 11, 1853), the governor was advised of this potentially explosive situation:

> I had several talks with different chiefs of Piedes, Pahvants; they said their hearts were good towards the Mormons and they wished to live in peace with them—said they were glad to have the Mormons come among them—said they were afraid of Walker [Walkara]—said he stole their children, and when he cannot steal them he will kill the parents and then take the children, and sell them to the Mexicans. From the best information that I could get, Walker is willing to live in peace, if he can have his own way in stealing other Indian children to sell them to the Mexicans, for guns and ammunition, or if we will buy these children of him to give him guns and ammunition to enable him to continue his robberies.

Mormon leaders now realized that the recently enacted legislation needed "teeth" before the persistent traders from New Mexico accepted the fact that Utah was an unhealthy place in which to ply their trade. To accomplish this aim, Brigham mobilized the Territorial Militia on April 23, 1853. William M. Wall now put down his *Book of Mormon* and cast aside his duties as missionary to take up the role of captain of a reconnaissance troop authorized by the governor. A detachment of thirty men was directed to proceed along the entire extent of Utah settlements, seeking out and seizing all traders, warning the Mormon settlers to be on their guard against these wandering merchants; and in general endeavoring to head-off any warfare which might erupt due to slave-taking activities.[12]

The mobilization of the militia created immediate problems. Slavery had been virtually legalized the previous year, and hence, could not be suppressed. The basis for the Mormon military reconnaissance, therefore was founded in the desire to stamp out the flow of contraband weapons and ammunition which were being brought into Utah by New Mexican traders. Brigham hoped that by curtailing the exchange of these essential trade items the slave traffic might be halted. Despite the governor's actions, the Mormons continued to be plagued by the commerce; and in fact, the Utes were demonstrating a belligerency heretofore unknown.

Walkara had welcomed the Saints with hopes that he could not only profit from any commerce with these new people, but could continue his commerce with New Mexicans as well. This Ute had urged Mormon expansion and settlement to the south of Salt Lake; and had even fed starving Mormon families during times of famine. Now Brigham had turned upon the "Hawk" like a rabid dog—severing the arteries which supplied his life blood. For years he had carried on the slave traffic with the New Mexicans—and Walkara was not to stop now. He still had enough warriors to teach Brigham a lesson. But like all conflicts with the Indians, a spark would be needed to touch off this holocaust. Walkara would patiently wait.

*   *   *

George McKenzie was well acquainted with the participants in the drama known as the Walker War; and he vividly recalled the incident which unleashed the wrath of Walkara and brought to the Mormons their bloodiest war:

Walker, the war chief of the Ute nation, with his braves and their families were encamped on Spring Creek about one mile north of the present town of Springville (Utah Co., Utah) all at peace with the white settlers, spending their time fishing and hunting, and trading and begging from the people. James Ivie, at that time had built a cabin, and was living in it with his wife and one child about half a mile north and west of where the Indians were camped. In the forenoon of July 17, 1853, an Indian and squaw came into Ivie's cabin. The squaw had three large trout which she wanted to trade to Mrs. Ivie for some flour. Flour being very scarce at that time, Mrs. Ivie called her husband in to get his views on the trade of that kind, he being at work digging a well. When he saw the trout, he said, 'They look mighty good to me,' and suggested that Mrs. Ivie might give three pints of flour for them, if the squaw would trade that way. He then went out of the cabin to resume his work.

Just after Ivie left two more Indians came into the cabin, one of whom seemed to be the husband or had some kind of claim on the squaw who had closed the trade with Mrs. Ivie. When this Indian saw the three trout, and the small amount of flour received in exchange, he became enraged and began beating the squaw, knocking her down, kicking and stomping her in a brutal manner. While this assault was being committed, Mrs. Ivie ran and called her husband. Mr. Ivie came to the cabin, and while the Indian was still beating the squaw, he took hold of the Indian and pulled him away, the squaw lying prostrate on the floor.

Ivie tried to push the Indian out of the cabin. When the Indian came, he left his gun standing by the door, and as Ivie pushed him out he grabbed his gun and tried to get in position to shoot Ivie. Ivie got hold of the muzzle of the gun, and in the struggle the gun was broken—the Indian retaining the stock and Ivie the barrel. When the gun broke, Ivie dealt the Indian a hard blow on the head with the barrel of the gun. The Indian fell to the ground, apparently dead, but did not expire until some hours later. The other Indian who came to the cabin the same time as his companion, drew his bow and arrow and shot Ivie, the arrow passing through the shoulder of Ivie's buckskin hunting shirt. At this time Ivie struck the Indian a violent blow and he fell unconscious by the side of the prostrate body of the other Indian. Just as Ivie got through with this second Indian, the squaw that he had been trying to protect came out of the cabin door with a stick of wood . . . With it she struck Ivie a blow in the face, cutting a deep gash in his upper lip, and the scar showed plainly from that time until his death.

Ivie again used the gun barrel to defend himself and struck the squaw. She fell unconscious by the side of the prostrate bodies of the two Indians.

At this stage in the drama Joseph Kelly, one of the foremost settlers of Springville, came upon the scene, and while looking at the three Indians lying apparently dead he was told by Ivie what had taken place. Kelly took a bucket of water that stood in the cabin and poured it on the Indians, trying to restore them. He then sent the Indian who first came to the cabin with the squaw for another bucket of water to try to restore the Indians to life; this Indian having taken no part in the trouble.

Kelly told Ivie to take his wife and child and go into town before the Indian camp was notified of the trouble, which he did.

The Indian that Kelly sent after the water went to the Indian camp and told of what had taken place at the Ivie cabin. The news of the trouble soon spread through the camp and the settlement ... Intense excitement reigned ...

Bishop Aaron Johnson, who was chief magistrate in all civil and military affairs at Springville, took immediate steps to protect the settlements. He ordered Caldwell's cavalry and Parry's infantry [militia companies] to be mustered in and be ready for action at call. All the other male citizens over sixteen years of age were enrolled as a home guard.

Johnson with his interpreter, William Smith, tried everything in their power to settle the trouble with Chief Walker, by offering ponies, beef, flour and blankets. But Walker refused to settle unless Ivie was given up to be tried by the Indians— which Johnson refused to do."[13]

The next day—July 18—Walkara broke camp and headed for the settlement of Payson, where he was joined by Arrapeen and his followers. Walkara and his *chaquetones* now struck hard and fast. In Payson Cañon they killed Alexander Keele; and left warning "that the war would last until the white people were all exterminated."

During the fall and summer of 1853, Walkara raided along the entire line of Mormon settlements. From Iron County in the far south of Utah, to Summit County north of Salt Lake—a distance of over 250 miles— Walkara's *chaquetones* struck. Nineteen Saints paid with their lives, and a number of smaller settlements were abandoned. Despite the call-up of militia— known as the Nauvoo Legion—Brigham remained essentially inactive. This has been a war of Walkara's choosing; and if the "Lion of Deseret" retaliated against the Utes, it would only intensify matters and prolong the conflict. Instead the order went forth for all Mormon communities to "fort-up." Towns that had previously stood exposed to the Indians were now walled. Even Salt Lake City was fortified with a parapet six feet high and six miles in extent.

By late November 1853, Walkara had tired of his war; and on the 28th of that month, Ammon, brother of the Ute chief, arrived at Parowan in southern Utah. A peace conference was proposed by the Utes. A formal council between Brigham and Walkara, however, did not take place until May 9th of the following year. S. N. Carvalho, chronicler of Colonel John C. Fremont's almost disastrous expedition across the Rockies in 1853-54, attended the peace-council between the Mormon leader and the "Hawk of the Mountains." Graphically he related the words and events that transpired at the meeting.

The imposing Walkara, attired in deer-skin hunting shirt appeared tired and haggard; and when he spoke it was as if a great burden had been released: "Wakara not wants to fight more. Wakara talk with great Spirit; Great Spirit say—'Make peace.' Wakara love Mormon chief; he is good man. When Mormon first come to live on Wakara's land, Wakara give him welcome. He give Wakara plenty bread, and clothes to cover his wife and children. Wakara no want to fight Mormon; Mormon chief very good man; he bring plenty oxen to Wakara. Wakara talk last night to Payede, to Kahutah, San Pete, Parvain—all Indian say, 'No fight Mormon or Merecats more.' If Indian kill white man again, Wakara make Indian howl."[14] Thus a council of Chicken Creek held on May 9 ended the Walker War—almost as abruptly as it had started. It was a war, like many other wars with western Indian tribes, brought on by an underlying cause—the slave traffic. And it seems almost ironic that at its close, Brigham Young would free two Indian children from the clutches of Walkara.

159

Again, Carvalho relates the incident which transpired shortly after conclusion of the peace-council:

> When I [Carvalho] returned I saw a crowd around the governor's wagon. I approached and found that his excellency had just concluded the purchase from the Utahs of two children, about two or three years of age. They were prisoners and infants of the Snake Indians, with whom the Utahs were at war. When the governor saw these deplorable objects, they were on the open, digging with their little fingers for grassnuts, or any roots to afford sustenance. They were almost living skeletons. They were usually treated in this way— that is, literally starved to death by their captors. Governor Young intended to have them sent to Salt Lake City, and have them cared for and educated like his own children. I never saw a more piteous sight than those two naked infants in bitter cold weather on the open snow, reduced by starvation to the verge of the grave—no, not the grave; for if they had died they would have been thrown on the common for the wolves to devour.[15]

* * *

Although the Walker War greatly shook the slave trade, it did not end it altogether. Various Paiute bands still lived in mortal terror of the swift incursions of slave raiders. In 1854 the Mormon missionary and "leather-stocking," Jacob Hamblin, encountered Piede Indians in the Santa Clara Valley who demonstrated great fear of the missionaries. Hamblin attributed this fear to the fact that his party had ridden into the Indian's country upon horseback and were armed in the same manner as were Ute and New Mexican raiders.[16] By mid-December 1854, Jacob Hamblin and his followers had begun to erect their mission headquarters which was destined to bloom into the town of Santa Clara.

Through long and tedious talks, and many smokes, Hamblin won the confidence of the Piedes and their neighbors, the Tonaquints. This Mormon missionary had shown the Indians that he was not a slave procurer, but was sent among them to learn their ways; and to instruct them in the doctrine of Mormonism. Jacob and his associates preached to the squaws against bartering off their children and extended the protecting hand of the Church in an attempt to halt the slave traffic in southern Deseret. The efforts of Hamblin, however, were futile. In the midst of this activity, Chief San Pete and his braves descended upon Santa Clara to purchase children from the Paiutes. Jacob watched helplessly as the Utes bartered with Piede squaws for their starving children. He was both amazed and horrified when he witnessed a Tonaquint brave release his daughter to a life of bondage for a gun and a horse. Discouraged and revolted by the scene, Hamblin wrote in his journal:

> I felt heartsick to see them [Tonaquint children] dragged from their homes to become slaves to the Gentiles. I saw the necessity of the elders doing all they could to ameliorate the condition of this miserable people . . .[17]

The task lying before the Saints, difficult as it might have seemed, was to be lightened. Already Walkara, the great Ute chief, was losing control over his band. Measles had ravaged the ranks of the *chaquetones*; and he, racked with pneumonia, was growing weak in mind and body. Sensing that death was near, the Hawk ordered his band northward to the land of his ancestors near Lake Timpanogos. However, at Meadow Creek, Walkara was too weak to continue his journey and his followers halted. On January 29, 1855, the greatest of Ute chiefs died.[18]

Word of Walkara's death traveled rapidly. Mormons and Indians alike worked fast to round up their stock and hide their children; for already the *chaquetones,* in compliance with their chief's last request, were scouring the region for the necessities for a burial befitting their leader. Walkara, with his last breath, had requested that his two squaws be killed and buried with him; and in the manner of the Navajos, that two Piede children be interred alive to herd the fifteen head of slaughtered horses in the after-life. He also requested that two Mormons be found to accompany him on his last great trek.[19]

Thus the death of Walkara eliminated one of the factors contributing to the slave trade in the Territory of Utah. Although the leadership of the *chaquetones* fell to Arrapeen, he was never the equal of his brother in plying the trade. In years that followed profits in the trade waned; and traders and procurers of human flesh thought twice before daring the threat to quick Mormon prosecution.

*   *   *

1. Kate B. Carter, *Indian Slavery of the West* (Salt Lake: 1938), p. 32.

2. Mormon historian, Peter Gottfredson, gives these additional details of this exchange of captives: "Soon after we moved on to our city lot . . ., a band of Indians camped near us. Early one morning we were excited at hearing their shrill, blood curdling war whoops, mingled with occasionally sharp cries of pain. Father sent me to the fort for help. Charley Decker and Barney Ward (the interpreter) and others hurried to the camp.

". . . Some of the braves had just returned from the war path. In a fight with 'Little Wolf's' band, they lost two men, but had succeeded in taking two girls prisoners. One of these they had killed and were torturing the other. To save her life Charley Decker bought her and took her to our house to be washed and clothed.

"She was the saddest looking piece of humanity I have ever seen. They had shingled her head with butcher knives and fire brands. All the fleshy parts of her body, legs and arms had been hacked with knives, then fire brands stuck into the wounds. She was gaunt with hunger and smeared from head to foot with blood and ashes." As told by John R. Young to Peter Gottfredson, and related in the latter's book, *History of Indian Depredations in Utah* (Salt Lake: 1919), pp. 16-17.

3. Ann & LeRoy Hafen, *The Old Spanish Trail,* p. 271.

4. In July 1850 the prefect of Abiquiu alone granted trade licenses to more than thirty individuals to operate among the Utes. See letter: James S. Calhoun to General Cyrus Choice, July 31, 1850: National Archives, New Mexico Superintendency of Indian Affairs Papers, Letters Received.

5. Such a license was granted on September 20, 1850 to slave-trader, José M. Chavez. This affidavit, issued by Superintendent Calhoun and approved by the military commandant at Abiquiu, Brevet Major L. P. Graham, granted Chavez the right to trade with the Utes in Utah Territory. With full knowledge as to this party's intent, the civil and military authorities granted the license with no mention of, nor restriction to the slave traffic. The Chavez license can be found in: National Archives; Records of the Office of Indian Affairs, Record Group No. 75; Records of the New Mexico Superintendency, Letters Received.

6. Apparently officials of the Office of Indian Affairs in New Mexico were in full sympathy with León. Indian Agent John Greiner wrote to the Commissioner of Indian Affairs on May 19, 1852, and defended the actions of León. The agent slated that the trader upon entering Utah had requested Brigham's permission to trade with the Utes but was "refused on the grounds that he was not a Mormon, but leave was granted him to trade with the Mormons." John Greiner to Luke Lea, May 19, 1852; National Archives; New Mexico Superintendency Papers, Letters Received.

7. Gwinn Harris Heap, *Central Route to the Pacific,* edited by Ann & LeRoy Hafen (Glendale: Arthur H. Clark Co., 1957), p. 207.

8. Daniel W. Jones, *Forty Years Among the Indians,* pp. 56-57.

9. National Archives: Office of Indian Affairs, Record Group No. 75; Utah Superintendency Papers, Letters Received.

10. *Ibid.*

11. *Journal History* (unpublished), in Church Historian's Office; Church of Jesus Christ of Latter-day Saints, Salt Lake City, Utah.

12. National Archives; Utah Superintendency Papers, Letters Received.

13. As quoted by Gottfredson, *Loc. cit.,* pp. 43-46.

14. S. N. Carvalho, *Incidents of Travel and Adventure in*

the Far West; wtih Col. Fremont's Last Expedition (New York: 1859), p. 193.

15. *Ibid.*, p. 194.

16. Paul Bailey, *Jacob Hamblin: Buckskin Apostle* (Los Angeles: Westernlore Press, 1948), p. 107.

17. As quoted from Hamblin journal, Dec. 2, 1854; in *ibid.*, pp. 109-110.

18. Bailey, *Walkara . . .*, p. 169.

19. *Ibid.*, p. 172.

SECTION FOUR

Victory
Over Tradition

I

With termination of the Civil War the nation could once again turn from problems of a strictly military nature to those facing the country as a whole. Turmoil stemming from maltreatment of the Indian now pressed for attention. In Washington there was growing suspicion that many Indian wars were provoked by "aggressions of lawless white men"; that the number of Indians were growing steadily less, due to disease "and treatment on the part of the whites—both by irresponsible persons and by government officials"; and by the ever-increasing encroachments of the westward movements upon the domain of these natives.

On March 3, 1865, a Joint Special Committee composed of members of both houses of Congress was appointed to inquire into these conditions. The work which this committee undertook was so immense—covering the problems of a continent—that holding of regular hearings were in many cases impossible. Instead, a circulating letter was sent to regular army officers, Indian agents and superintendents—inquiring into their knowledge of Indian affairs.

167

The Joint Special Committee was split into three divisions; and its chairman, James R. Doolittle of Wisconsin; Lafayette S. Foster, Vice President of the United States; and Lewis W. Ross of Illinois were assigned New Mexico, Utah, Colorado, Indian Territory and the State of Kansas.[1] The Doolittle Committee —as the Joint Special Committee would be known— began its work at Fort Leavenworth on May 17; and by July 4 it had extended its investigations to New Mexico Territory. A short hearing in Santa Fe and the collecting of numerous reports from military and civil authorities revealed the depths of New Mexican Indian troubles. For the first time in the history of the territory, real causes of the Navajo wars were beginning to come to the surface. The investigation revealed the fact that for generations slave raids had been conducted against the Navajos by Mexicans—which only resulted in retaliation by the Diné.

Henry Connelly, Governor of New Mexico, ex-trader and resident of the southwest for over forty years, reported that "Navajos made forays to take sheep and stock, killing all who made resistance—their object seeming rather to plunder, especially flocks and herds, than a desire to take life by attacking towns and villages. The Mexicans generally have been on the defensive. But sometimes they go after them to make reprisals, to get back their own, and to get what more they could. They mutually also captured and held as slaves the women and children of each other." In summation, Governor Connelly stated, "I believe the Mexicans captured the most children, the Indians the most herds."[2]

Military commandant and instigator of the "Long Walk" of the Navajos, Brigadier General James H. Carleton, substantiated the words of the territorial governor: "With the exception of one or two intervals of a few years each, there has been a constant state of hostility between the people of New Mexico and the Navajo Indians. Even in these intervals occasional forays were made into their country to recapture the stolen stock, and they would kill some of the Indians and capture some of the women and children and make slaves of them. But in times when open hostilities existed these efforts were increased on each side to capture stock and women and children, so that the country was kept in a continued state of commotion."[3]

Louis Kennon, a native of Georgia and a physician by profession, had been in the Territory of New Mexico for twelve years prior to the Doolittle investigations —and during those years had ample opportunity to observe the manner in which natives were treated; and he formed some definite opinions as to Indian affairs.

"I think the Navajos have been the most abused people on the continent," tersely wrote Kennon. ". . . in all hostilities the Mexicans have always taken the initiative with but one exception that I know of. When I first came here the Navajos were at peace, and had been a long time. There was a pressure brought to bear upon the commander of the department by the Mexicans, and all Americans who pandered to that influence to make war upon the Navajos. General Garland was commander of the department at that time, and if you asked the Mexicans any reason for making war, they would give no other reason, but that the Navajos had a great many sheep and horses and a great many children."[4]

The Doolittle Committee had at last brought to public attention the fact that Indian slavery was indeed an underlying cause of many conflicts between red and white men in the arid southwest. For years slave raiders had penetrated Indian country, and captives brought back were auctioned off as if they were livestock. To such an extent had this practice prevailed, that thousands of women and children were held as servants in New Mexican homes.[5]

Previous to the Civil War, the price of these menials varied from $75 to $150; but with increased military concentration and the establishment of Bosque Redon-

to Chief Justice Kirby Benedict, Navajo captives now being auctioned off for $400 apiece;[6] and many people holding these menials were the most respected citizens in territorial affairs. The judge further pointed out that these individuals were alarmed at the rising interest in the Indian slavery question—brought on in large measure by the Doolittle Committee's investigations—and were fearful of court action. Benedict's report accused the family of Governor Henry Connelly and Superintendent of Indian Affairs, Felipe Delgado, of holding Indians in slavery. Even Associate Justice Hubbell was accused of selling an Indian woman.[7] General Carleton's report to the committee substantiated Benedict's claims, and added the detail that many leading citizens objected to the establishment of the Navajo reservation at Bosque Redondo—because it would put a stop to slave raiding. New Mexicans were also fearful, Carleton claimed, that a cut in military forces would ensue, thus reducing the millions of dollars annually expended in the territory.[8]

The systems of servitude prevalent in the American Southwest—peonage and Indian slavery—was not affected by the Emancipation Proclamation, as both were never regarded as involuntary servitude, as in the case of Negro slavery. Peonage was recognized in the territory by the "Law Regulating Contracts between Masters and Servants," passed by the legislative assembly in 1858-59. This special act provided that a peon receive a wage of five dollars a month, with which he was expected to provide for his family. Since he drew all his subsistence from his master, the peon's debts continually grew until a life of servitude invariably resulted. Among New Mexicans no distinction was made between peonage and the enslavement of Indians. Both were considered as voluntary servitude in the status of the territory—and in the traditional way of thinking. But a distinction was very apparent, even to the most casual of observers. Peons were not bought and sold as

170

chattel but Indians, particularly Navajos, Apaches, and Paiutes were traded as if they were swine or sheep.

Slave owning might be expected to be confined only to the wealthy families of New Mexico. This was not the case, however, for any householder who could raise $150. He could purchase an Indian captive—and many individuals had four or five. Estimates of Indian captives in the territory, at the time of the Civil War, varied from as few as 500 to as many as 6,000. It was claimed that in Santa Fe alone, 500 Navajos were held in bondage. The estimate of 6,000 may approach the truth. Ethnohistorian David Brugge has recorded some 790 Navajo baptismals alone, for the decade of the 1860s. But whatever the number of captives, it is apparent that many of the prominent and influential citizens of the territory were leading slave holders. Governors, federal officials, and even Indian Agents and Superintendents, owned Indian menials.

The legality of the system of peonage and Indian slavery was closely analyzed by the Doolittle Committee. Summoning his legal knowledge, Justice Benedict reported that he knew "of no law in this territory by which property in Navajo or other Indian can be recognized in any person whatever, any more than property can be recognized in the freest white man or black man." In several court proceedings, the judge reported, he had tried to uphold his conviction. In 1855, while the district court was convened in Valencia County, a *habeas corpus* case was brought before his bench by a wealthy woman. She claimed possession of a Navajo girl, then twelve years of age, whom she had held for seven years. Benedict judged the girl to be free. But such cases were few in New Mexico at that time. Although the courts—at least those of Benedict's—were available to the Indian menial or peon, they were usually so intimidated by their masters, and the conditions under which they lived, that few, if any, sought legal aid.[9]

* * *

To all outward appearance the investigations of the Doolittle Committee brought little if any improvement to chaotic Indian affairs in New Mexico. Once back in Washington, the committee began the tedious task of sifting through the mass of collected data. To make its investigations even more thorough, and thus give a clearer insight into problems confronting the administration of Indian Affairs, Doolittle requested the Department of Interior to undertake still another survey. Therefore, in 1865, the Office of Indian Affairs appointed Julius K. Graves special agent to the New Mexico Superintendency of Indian Affairs—and authorized him to delve still further into the nefarious practice of Indian slavery.

Upon reaching New Mexico in December 1865, Graves methodically began probing the depths of turmoil created during past generations of relations between red and white men. His findings substantiated what the Doolittle Committee had discovered—that many of the conflicts with tribes were directly related to the practice of securing Indian slaves. In his "Report Number 11,"[10] Graves informed the Commissioner of Indian Affairs that peonage had existed in the territory for more than a century, and "was the universal recognized mode of securing labor and assistance—and the results of that system were identical to that of Negro slavery as formerly practiced in the southern states."

Two forms of peonage, reported Graves, existed in the southwest: that of voluntary servitude from the poorer classes; and that derived solely from captive Indians, usually women and children taken during forays against hostile tribes. In the former case, the peon became indebted and worked his debt out at the "paltry recompense of from $2 to $15 per month," which invariably resulted in a life of bondage, as the debt always increased. In the latter case, the Indian captive was compelled to toil without recompense of any kind.

172

Both systems, surmised the special agent, originated in the Mexican states of Chihuahua, Coahuila and Nueva León.

Graves, like Doolittle, found that Indians were held in bondage in truly large numbers—thus adding truth to Chief Justice Benedict's words. According to the agent's estimates, there were "about 400 Indian peons in Santa Fe, and more than double that number throughout the rest of the territory. They were held by all classes of citizens; however, the most were possessed by the people of ease and affluence, who have in some instances upwards of a dozen . . ." Nearly every government official in the territory sustained Indian slavery—and their arguments for it, insisted Graves, were identical to those used in behalf of Negro slavery. In spite of stringent orders prohibiting slavery, nearly every federal officer in New Mexico held Indian menials. The Superintendent of Indian Affairs, claimed the special agent, possessed half a dozen; and those officials who did not practice peonage, sanctioned it by protecting those individuals who held Indian menials.[11]

The treatment of Indian slaves, conceded Graves, varied of course with the temperament of their masters. "I have witnessed these unfortunate beings under various relations—in some cases these people probably are better off by reason of their bondage, being secure of a home, than they would be otherwise; while in by far the greater number of cases their plight cannot but excite our pity."

Graves saw that the system of Indian slavery, if persisted in, would lead only to conflict with the tribes: "The natural tendencies of the peonage system with special reference to the 'captive' are as you will readily admit, calculated to keep alive the Indian troubles, and indeed, provoke the savage beings to continued acts of vengeance; and hence, laying aside all the promptings of humanity, the system should be immediately broken up as tending to demoralize, not only the people and

173

the Indians, but endangering the peace, security and welfare of the territory ..."

Graves sided with the Indians against those who viewed the red man as a being possessing little, if any, feelings for his family and children. "The Indian is endowed with the *same* attributes of *justice, love* and *affection* that pertains to the civilized world—and when robbed of his children, he cannot but experience the deepest sorrow—added to this loss, the reflection that those children are beyond his reach and guided by his untutored sense of wrong, the Indian is speedily nerved to brave his life against his enemy; and then that his deeds are characterized by the most brutal atrocities that man can describe or the mind conceive." There was only one course to follow in respect to Indian bondage, Graves felt. The Government should at once adopt vigorous measures to bring about its immediate abolition; and an agency such as the Freedmen's Bureau established to care and protect those Indians reclaimed from bondage.[12]

* * *

After the Civil War, men of national prominence believed that the Emancipation Proclamation was all embracing, including white, black—and red peoples. When the investigations of the Doolittle Committee and Special Agent J. K. Graves revealed that slavery was still very much alive in the southwest, the ship of state was violently rocked. In late spring of 1865, "Free Soiler" and ardent reconstructionist, Senator Charles Sumner of Massachusetts, delivered from the floor of Congress a speech denouncing the evils of Indian slavery. In this virulent speech, the senator condemned General James Carleton and Territorial Governor Henry Connelly for allowing the practice to persist. Indian slavery, long rooted in New Mexican tradition, had become a national issue.

Throughout summer of 1865 reports and recommendations were made on the subject in Washington. The Department of the Interior, Office of Indian Affairs, and the War Department could no longer turn their backs upon the insidious practice. President Andrew Johnson was drawn into the fray and immediately issued orders to all government employees to turn their attentions to the abolishment of Indian bondage:

> It is represented to me in a communication from the Secretary of the Interior that Indians in New Mexico have been seized and reduced into slavery; and it is recommended that the authority of the Executive branch of the Government should be exercised for the effectual suppression of a practice which is alike in violation of the rights of the Indians, and the provisions of the Organic law of said Territory.
>
> Concurring in this recommendation I do hereby order that the heads of the several Executive Departments do enjoin upon their subordinates, agents and employes under their respective orders, or supervision in that Territory, to discontinue the practice aforesaid, and to take all lawful means to suppress the same.[13]

In obedience to the President's dictum, Secretary of the Interior James Harlan and William P. Dole, Commissioner of Indian Affairs, advised their subordinates in New Mexico—many of whom owned Indian slaves —to at once take the necessary steps to put "and end to this barbarious and inhuman practice."[14]

In the Territory of New Mexico, the exposure of Indian bondage created a political bombshell that exploded not only in Santa Fe but in the national capital as well. The New Mexican delegate to Congress, José Francisco Chavez, climbed on Senator Sumner's bandwagon. A slave owner himself, Chavez hypocritically leveled allegations at Connelly and Carleton, accusing these men of letting the practice persist through the organization of the Navajo Campaign of 1863-64. A few people in the Territory, however, rushed to the defense; and on February 2, 1867, these accusations were answered by an open letter in the pro-Carleton Santa Fe *Gazette*:

General Carleton and Governor Connelly and those who have cooperated with them in New Mexico, have uniformly and persistently done all they could have done to break up the trade in Indian captives, and if they have not done as much as you gentlemen of the east think . . . you ought to take into consideration the difficulties . . . by which they were surrounded.

The *Gazette* next leveled an attack at Chavez. He was charged with retaining more peons and Indian slaves than any other household in the territory; and his mother's family was also accused of holding peons. Together, it was charged, the Chavez family exerted an almost insurmountable obstacle to overcoming the insidious practice.[15]

The evils of Indian slavery had at least been exposed —and in Washington the wheels of justice began to turn. On March 2, 1867, Congress passed an act to abolish and "Forever prohibit the system of Peonage in the Territory of New Mexico and other parts of the United States." This inclusive act renounced all traditions, laws, and orders permitting bondage which had persisted since the days of the Spanish, and set severe penalties for violators. The new law, however, served only to draw people's attention to the evil—it liberated few if any slaves. In Santa Fe, on June 10, 1868, acting Governor Herman H. Heath, proclaimed via a circular his recognition of the newly passed act, and reiterated the penalties awaiting those persons still holding slaves and peons. Heath also requested the aid of all civil officers and "all true and loyal citizens" of the Territory in stamping out this "crime against mankind." Still people tenaciously held to their traditional system of slavery. During the decade of the 1860s nearly 800 Navajos had been baptized in territorial churches. In the southern Colorado counties of Conejos and Costillo federal investigation revealed another 145 Indians held in servitude. Of these 110 were Navajos—taken during the years 1862-64; 8 were Paiutes, and 15 were Apache. The remaining individuals were of other tribal affiliations.[16] It was clear that more drastic measures would have to be resorted to if the goals of the Congressional and Territorial laws were to be reached.

The deciding measure was adopted on July 27, 1868, when Congress passed Joint Resolution No. 65. This resolution invested power in the hands of a man capable of bringing swift results—the commanding general of the United States Army. Lieutenant General William T. Sherman now was authorized to use the most efficient means at his disposal to reclaim from bondage the women and children of the Navajo, as well as other tribes, then held in bondage; and return them to their respective reservations.[17]

The actions of Congress had a profound effect on the citizens of New Mexico. Thousands of Indians were held throughout the territory, many by prominent families who would resist any Congressional attempt to liberate their "property." When the United States District Attorney was directed to commence grand jury investigations, three hundred witnesses were subpoenaed from Taos, Santa Fe, and Rio Arriba Counties. The hearings were a fiasco—those witnesses owning Indian slaves declined to testify; the grand jurors themselves owned Indians and were not sympathetic to the proceedings; and those personally affected by the hearings mustered their last energies to withstand the military and civil investigations. Finally, on August 6 the Santa Fe *New Mexican* published a "humanitarian plea" in answer to General Sherman and the court sessions:

. . . the Navajos are a savage and barbarous people. These captives from this tribe have now for years lived among civilized people; have learned the language of the country, have become christianized—all being Catholics; and their habits have become those of the civilized race among whom they dwell, and one in fifty of them desire to leave their civilized life for a renewal of the barbarous and uncivilized life of their tribe. They prefer a life among our people to one among their own. They are free—they may hire to any person whom they may please to serve; but it is certain, that, constituted as they are most if not all of these who come under the classification of "Navajo captives," prefer to remain in homes where they have so long been domesticated, and where they possess the advantages not only of religion, but of civilized life . . . It becomes then a serious question of humanity, whether those Navajos who are now voluntarily living among our people . . . shall be forced back upon savage life against their will . . . or whether, by voluntary action they shall remain as they are, the objects of care by the church and civil protection by the Territory.[18]

General Sherman did not heed this plea, and from his St. Louis headquarters ordered Major General George W. Getty, commander of the District of New Mexico, to convey to the Navajos the intentions of the Army to comply with the recently-passed laws "in justice to the women and children affected." Sherman further urged that should any of the tribe desire to search for relatives held in bondage, Getty would permit them and provide for it out of Army funds; and act as guardian for any women and children that may be returned and see that they reached their tribe in safety.[19]

* * *

1. For additional details as to the duty of the Doolittle Committee consult: L. R. Bailey, *The Long Walk: A History of the Navajo Wars* (Los Angeles: Westernlore Press, 1964).

2. *Condition of Tribes,* p. 332.

3. *Ibid.,* p. 323.

4. *Ibid.,* pp. 333-334.

5. Estimates of Indian slaves held throughout the Territory of New Mexico ran as high as 5,000. Santa Fe alone was credited with having 1,000 Indian menials.

6. *Condition of Tribes,* pp. 225-226.

7. *Ibid.*

8. *Ibid.,* p. 324.

9. *Ibid.,* p. 326.

10. All of J. K. Graves' report may be found in the New Mexico Superintendency papers, 1866.

11. *Annual Report of Commissioner of Indian Affairs, 1866,* p. 137.

12. See Report No. 40 by J. K. Graves in *Ibid.,* pp. 133-134.

13. Proclamation by President Andrew Johnson (dated June 9, 1865), in Records of the New Mexico Superintendency, Letters received from Commissioners, 1864-65.

14. James Harlan to William P. Dole, June 12, 1865; *Ibid.,* Letters received from Commissioners, 1864.

15. Santa Fe *Gazette,* February 2, 1867.

16. For tabulation of captives see Lafayette Head to John Evan, July 17, 1865; New Mexico Superintendency Papers, 1865.

17. Consult L. R. Bailey, *The Long Walk,* pp. 231-232.

18. Santa Fe *New Mexican,* August 6, 1868.

19. *Ibid.*

II

Thousands of words have been written outlining the history of Indian depredations in the trans-Pecos southwest. But for that area there exists only a comparatively small body of literature devoted to Indian captivity—one of the primary causes of turmoil. And there is even less literature explaining effects which years of captivity had upon the individual. It is easy to say that so many Mexican women and children were carried off by marauding Indians, or that so many Apaches, Navajos, and Paiutes were taken by Spanish or Mexican expeditions. But what these captives endured is another story—a story which must, of necessity, come from the individuals.

Captivity—be it with Indians or Spanish—had profound and far-reaching effects upon the individual. From church records, correspondence of military officers and Indian agents, can be gleaned the idea of the number of captives, their tribal or national origin, and eventual fate. Equally, can it be demonstrated the medium of barter reflected in the slave traffic. But the cir-

181

cumstances surrounding initial abduction and what happened to these individuals is a story in itself.

The effects of captivity are an exceedingly difficult problem to study—for it involves the fate of persons who have been torn from their own society and eventually enter an often totally alien group. Dr. A. Irving Hallowell, Professor of Anthropology at the University of Pennsylvania, is one of few students to delve into the significance of Indian captivity. Realizing that no conceptionalized framework existed with which to tackle this problem, Hallowell coined the term—*transculturalization.*

This rather formidable word implies a concept having universal applications, for it is simply "the process whereby individuals under a variety of circumstances are temporarily or permanently detached from one group, enter the web of social relations that constitute another society, and come under the influence of its customs, ideas, and values to a greater or lesser degree. A correlative term, *transculturite,* can be used to designate those individuals who have undergone transculturalization."

Although this concept has wide application—including any individual who passes from one society to another—when applied to Indian captives a number of variables affecting the degree of readjustment must be taken into consideration. Age of the captive, length of residence with the receptor society, attitudes of both captive and individuals of alien group, and the nature of roles enacted—are all factors having a direct bearing upon how complete the readjustment will be. In many cases the transition was superficial, producing little if any psychological impact upon basic manners, attitudes and values. On the other hand, the transformation may have been so complete as to eradicate every vestige of former traits, the individual eventually becoming completely identified with the second culture.

However, it was not the anthropologist who first speculated upon the adjustment process involved in

182

Hallowell's term, "transculturalization." At an early date there were in the arid southwest men such as Captain John C. Cremony—men who were well aware of the conditions under which the Indian captive lived. Cremony, an officer attached to the United States-Mexican boundary survey, and later served conspicuously on the frontier, had numerous opportunities to observe the treatment of captives. In his book, *Life Among the Apaches,* this officer related his views regarding the "adjustment process" experienced by Mexican women held by Apache bands:

. . . there is but modicum of difference between the actual condition of the women in the northern frontiers of Mexico and that of the Apaches. In each case it is she who does all the work, and undergoes all the servitude to which women are condemned among semicivilized races. In the second place, after having borne children for an Apache [the captive's] . . . affections are concentrated upon her offspring more than upon the savage author of their birth, and she will not abandon them under almost any circumstances. In the third place she knows that her restrained and protracted residence among the Apaches would subject her to rude, unhuman and opprobrious comments among her fellow countrywomen—should she return . . . It is therefore natural for a Mexican woman to cling to her captivity in preference to returning to her native peoples.[2]

Although reflecting current Anglo-American biases, Cremony nevertheless was right. There was but a shade of difference between the life led by many Mexicans to that of an Apache. The vicissitudes of life experienced by Mexicans in Sonora and Chihuahua was not much different from that faced by Apaches and Comanches. In fact, the necessities of life might be more plentiful in the camps of Indians than upon the large ranches of

183

the landed gentry. The peon, and the life of servitude which he led, was little above that of bondage to the Indian. Thus the young captain alludes to the primary factors determining the degree of transculturalization— that is, the nature and compatibility of value systems, which taken with the factor of time, sets the stage for complete transition. This phenomena in its entirety, can be seen repeatedly when the historical record and ethnological data are consulted. Nearly all captives— whether taken by Indians or Mexicans—were small children; and if not promptly restored, quickly adopted alien ways, even to the extent of losing all semblance of their former language and customs.

The military man, however, was not alone in his postulations relative to the socialization of captives. Perhaps the real depth of study has been by men who would be classified by scholars as being unfit for such undertakings—for their approach is not scientific, but dramatic. It has been the novelist who has truly searched for the effects of captivity; and vividly has this artist portrayed it. Alan LeMay, in a 1956 novel *The Searchers,* graphically outlines the nightmare of bondage among South Plains tribes; and the unrelenting pursuit to free a ten-year-old girl from the horrors of captivity. Will Cook's *Comanche Captives* probes the psychological depths of captivity. In this latter work a true ring is heard in the captive's reply to demands of restitution, that "I am a Comanche!"[3] These are words not unlike those spoken and recorded in countless entries in the correspondence of the Office of Indian Affairs.

In 1859 several Mexicans stolen at an early age from Rio Grande settlements were brought into Fort Defiance by their Navajo abductors. These individuals were now Indian in every sense of the word; and when given the choice of returning to their Mexican families or remaining with the Indians, they chose the latter. They had lived as Indians so long that they had lost the Spanish speech and considered the vermilion mesas and

184

cañons of Navajoland their true home. When offered freedom, one captive replied, "the Navajos were his brothers and his friends, and with them he desired to live."[4]

The archives of the Arizona Pioneers' Historical Society, in Tucson, contains a number of accounts useful in ferreting out the readjustment process undergone by captives. An old army scout, Apache Bill, reminisced considerably about his life among the Apaches, the circumstances of his abduction, treatment received from the Indians, and the depth of transition from one culture to another.

Apache Bill, whose real name was William H. Young, was born in Philadelphia, January 17, 1844. His father was John Young, and Bridget Burton was his mother. In 1852 young William started west with a family by the name of Howard to visit his uncle in Fort Worth, Texas. In his own words, Apache Bill recounted that

after a short stay at Fort Worth, we joined a party of immigrants on their way to California.

We struck the old Santa Fe Trail to New Mexico, then we traveled southwest, coming through Cow Springs, then on into Arizona. It was while we were camped at the Vinaterilla Ranch near Tres Alamos on the San Pedro River, about nine miles north of where Benson is now . . . when a pack of Apache Indians started to raid our camp. I was playing about two or three hundred feet away from the wagons, when I saw the Indians driving off our stock; scared, I started to run as fast as I could to the wagons, where the men had opened fire on the Indians. As I was running I heard horses' hoofs beating the ground close behind me, then as I saw a horse almost over me, at the same instant someone grabbed me by the back of the shirt and swung me around and up and sat me astride of his horse right in front of him; a big

185

buck Apache Indian, his horse going at full speed he headed for the brush and foothills. After several days traveling with them, we came to what appeared to be a permanent camp in the Chiricahua Mountains. There they turned me over to the squaws whom I helped pack wood and water and helped them with their tanning of hides; I fell into their customs, and was always a willing worker and the squaws named me 'Nalapi Enchos,' (meaning good friend, in the Apache language).

After I had been under the care of the squaws for about a year and a half, I now could speak Apache, I was then about 10 years old. The bucks began to teach me the use of the bow and arrow and to ride horses; shortly afterwards they began to take me out on their marauding trips: I would hold their horses while they would plunder the immigrants trains, and on several of these expeditions they would kill all the immigrants, and what provisions they could not carry off, they would destroy.

I made a number of trips in southern Arizona, New Mexico and northern Mexico. They had a few firearms, which they guarded with a great deal of care, mostly of the flintlock variety. These they had taken from the immigrants that they raided.

We lived most of the while in the field on raw beef, venison, jerky and pinole (parched wheat or corn ground to a flour on rocks called a metate) . . . When we returned from our raiding trips, the squaws would prepare different kinds of dishes. They would take the young tender shoots from the cactus of the tuna variety, and fry or boil them in earthen dishes, and it makes a palatable dish . . . They also make a gruel out of mesquite beans they call atoli. That is also palatable; and a preserve they call sopichi from the giant cactus, the sahuaro, that resembles or tastes like the fig.

I dressed in a G-string and a pair of buckskin

moccasins that reached to my knees. For those who have not seen one, I will explain how to put on a G-string: You first place a buckskin belt or cord around the naked waist. Then you take a piece of cloth 8 to 12 inches wide, and 6 to 7 feet long (according to your height); place end No. 1 of cloth under belt or cord in front, pulling it down till the other end, No. 2, comes to your knees. You bring end No. 1 between your crotch, up your back, under the belt or cord in the middle of your back and pull up the cloth snug, and you then have on what is called a G-string. To complete the picture, put on a pair of buckskin moccasins that extend to knees or hips, then trim your hair just below the ears almost to the shoulders all the way around, then wrap a cloth around the head, parting the hair in the center, and place the hair to the right and left of your eyes, the cloth holding the hair in place, and you have the field dress of an Apache Indian.

These Indians made their headquarters in the Chiricahua Mountains at what is called the Horse Shoe Bend. Raton and Miguel Tuerto (blind in one eye) were the leaders of these outlaws, who were called the Coyoteros. Most of the depredations done were by renegade and outlaw Apaches, breaking away from the main tribe, they would go on these marauding expeditions killing here and there whenever they found their prey unguarded, and taking what plunder they could carry off.

In the fall of 1858 we were in a marauding expedition in northern Sonora, Mexico, and were driving what stock we had north to the Chiricahua Mountains. We made camp about ten or twelve miles east of Fronteras and near Pesqueria's Ranch. We knew the Mexicans were on our trail, but thought we had thrown them off. That night they quietly surrounded us while we were asleep, and waited for daylight. When the first Indian got up, the shooting started—we were taken completely by surprise. I hid in a clump of catclaws till the shooting was over. A number of Indians had escaped through the dense undergrowth. As some Mexicans came close to me, I came out from under cover and walked towards them. They were about to fire on me when they noticed I was white and had light hair. They lowered their rifles, they spoke to one another, then walked up to me and spoke to me in Spanish. I could not understand them. They saw I was not an Indian and they took me to Fronteras, where I was turned over to a Mexican by the name of Elias. He showed me the greatest of consideration, and did everything in his power to make it pleasant for me.

I was thoroughly cleaned, and I certainly needed to be. My G-string was replaced by a pair of pants, my hair trimmed, now I was fairly presentable; in the meantime they found a man who could speak English. Seeing that I was white and of the Anglo Saxon race, he spoke to me in English. I could not understand him. I had forgotten my own language; they later got an Apache interpreter, and I told my story from the time I had been taken at the Vinaterilla Ranch on the San Pedro River, Arizona, a little over six years before. I was now close to 15 years of age and quite husky, as I could scuffle any of the younger bucks and ride as well . . .

After a stay of about three weeks with Don Elias at Fronteras, Sonora, Manuel Gallego and four other Mexicans started with me to Fort Buchanan, Arizona. After four days travel we arrived, and I was turned over to the commander of the post, who was Major Ewell of the 1st Dragoons. After a day's rest, the Mexicans returned to Fronteras. I loathed to see them go.

Through an Apache interpreter, I retold my

story to Major Ewell. I had forgotten my first name, but I still had a faint recollection of Young, [which] I pronounced . . . Yung . . . Major Ewell instantly knew that I was the missing son of John Young who had served under General Scott in Mexico; and who had sent notice to all detachments . . . on duty in Arizona and New Mexico to be on the lookout for me, as no trace had been found of my death. He wrote to my father who was in Philadelphia, of me being captured by the Mexicans and turned over to him. In the meantime, the troopers had taken interest in me and were teaching me to speak English—and it all came back to me like a dream.

During the next five or six months, the troops were called out to do scout duty and I was permitted to go along. I felt different with my new clothes, boots, coat, pants, shirt and hat—the first in nearly seven years. They felt clumsy at first, but I was very much taken up with my uniform. My food also was so different, eating bread, beans, bacon, cooked beef, coffee and sugar and vegetables. While I was with the Apaches, it was straight jerky or raw beef and once in awhile pinole.

* * *

In the spring of 1859, I was put in care of Lieutenant Longstreet, who was paymaster of this district at the time. He brought me as far as Yuma, Arizona and turned me over to troops that were going to San Francisco, California. Our trip to San Francisco was uneventful. After several days wait for a vessel, I was put on the sailing vessel *Tuscorora* bound for New York . . . After several months sailing, I cannot say how long exactly, we reached New York. My father had been notified overland what boat I had taken, and he met me in New York and drove me to Philadelphia by buggy, where my mother was overcome with joy.

After several days, I was put in school until the year of 1862, I enlisted in the 95th Penn. Vol. Inf. Not being of age, my mother secured my discharge. In February 23, 1863, I again enlisted, this time in Company "K," 3rd Penn. Heavy Artillery, under the name of W. H. Burton, using my mother's maiden name. In March 1864, I was transferred to 188th Penn. Inf., and served in this regiment until the end of the war, and was mustered out by general orders.

Understanding the Apache language, I was sent to Carlisle, Pennsylvania, and enlisted as Apache Scout and interpreter and was attached to Troop "C," 1st U.S. Cavalry; and entered into the campaign against the Apache Indians . . ."[5]

The strange wild lives which individuals like Apache Bill led have been the theme for a number of novels. But regardless of how well their existence lends itself to fictionalized accounts, a thread of truth and similarity is seen when case histories are compared. Due to economics of trade, as well as tribal property concepts, usually all were taken captive when very young. Plunder, either in the form of mules or captives, was the prerequisite in any exchange for weapons, powder, lead, and liquor—all essential for maintenance of raiding practices, if not the very incentive to pillage. Older captives, therefore, would never bring market value, but women and children under the age of eighteen, could be traded at a profit. When the trade in captives and livestock was at its height—between 1840 and 1855—female captives were most highly prized by marauding tribes; and for that matter the Mexicans. But when the trade waned during the latter year of the Indian wars, and disposal of contraband became more difficult, Indians were more inclined to retain their captives. At this time preference switched from females to males—probably due to the feeble attempt to maintain tribal strength.[8]

During the latter half of the 19th century numerous cases come to light of Mexicans and Anglo-Americans being retained by Indian bands. The central theme of all these histories is one of readjustment from one culture to another. When abduction occurred at an early age, and confined to an Indian camp year after year, these individuals slowly became "Indianized," or to use Hallowell's term, they were "transculturites." Gradually they lost their former language, and ways of their past grew dim in their memories, being replaced by Indian traits. If confinement with an alien society had been of sufficient length to have displaced all previous traits—as in the case of Apache Bill—readjustment to "freedom" was often a difficult if not impossible task.

In the eyes of Anglo-Americans the process of becoming "Indianized" was considered a retrograde step. Therefore, an individual attempting to resume a role in his former society was often an object of contempt and scorn—they would always be identified with Indians. The ex-captive and the squaw man bore the brunt of ostracism. "They had plunged into the deepest pit of social degradation."[9] Those individuals redeemed from bondage often lived in a twilight world, that was neither Indian nor white man. Nearly all male captives held by Apaches and Navajos never quite made the transition. Without exception they became intermediaries between red and white men. Some served as army scouts and helped carry the war to the camps of their abductors. Still others were interpreters and rendered invaluable aid—as at the peace parleys conducted by Generals George Crook and Oliver O. Howard. Regardless of the roles assumed and how they were viewed by contemporaries, the ex-captives are the unsung heroes of the Indian wars.

Another captive around whom has grown considerable legend is Marajildo Grijalva—and like his peers, he could never shed the shackles of bondage—and In-

191

dianization. A prominent scout under the command of General Crook during the Apache campaigns of 1870s and 1880s, this Mexican was born about 1840, at Bacuachi, Sonora. This pueblo and its neighboring villages lay in the path of Apache raiding; and frequently were hard hit by marauding Indians heading deep into interior Sonora.

In the spring of 1850 Chiricahua Apaches under Miguel Narbona pushed deep into Mexico, approaching the limits of Arispe. Raiding surrounding villages, the Indians did not spare Bacuachi. Marajildo and his brother, Francisco, were herding their family's sheep when Apaches launched their attack. The flock was a prime target, for it offered subsistence to the rapidly moving Indians. Sweeping down upon the prize, the Indians slaughtered many of the animals and captured the two *pastores*.

Kept under close surveillance, the Grijalva brothers rode with the Indians during their Sonoran foray, and returned with them to the Chiricahua Mountains, in present-day southeastern Arizona. It was there that the young captives served their apprenticeship to the Apaches. They were placed under the direction of squaws, performing menial chores about the Indian camp. Slowly they fell into the ways and tradition of the Apaches—they had literally "traded breeches for breach-cloth." It was then, that the boys received training from the family that claimed them, in the arts of warfare and the hunt—all basic knowledge to any Apache.

For nearly nine years Marajildo served the Indians, and his training was rigorous. He could now stalk game as well as any Apache. His muscles were sinewed from constant training in physical combat with boys his age and older. He had approached the age where he would Poston records that the captive "was at the Overland Mail station at Steen's Peak, when the Apaches went in take his place as a warrior. Marajildo was in his teens when he saw his first Anglo-American. Charles D.

there to see the Americans and make a treaty. They afterwards came to Fort Buchanan . . . on the Sonoita, and saw Captain Ewell . . ., who was in command there."

Shortly thereafter, in 1859, Marajildo escaped from the Apaches. He sought sanctuary at Fort Thorn, New Mexico; and was employed as interpreter to Dr. Michael Steck, then Apache Agent. In 1863 he served General West, commander of the newly organized Department of Arizona; and upon establishment of Fort Bowie, served its garrison as interpreter and scout for nearly four years.

With termination of his duties at Apache Pass the ex-captive moved rapidly around Arizona. In the years to come he appears at nearly every scene of action with the Apaches. From Bowie, Marajildo went to Camp Wallen, remaining there two years; then back to Fort Bowie for the latter phases of the Apache campaigns. It was at this post in Apache Pass that the Mexican was employed by General George Crook, whom he served until conclusion of the Apache roundup.

Grijalva's story, however, does not stop here. About the same time that he was captured by Apaches (1850), a young girl was carried from the Sonoran village of Chinape, close to Bacuachi. Perhaps she was captured by the same band which abducted Marajildo and his brother. Rosa Jorquez was traded from one band of Apaches to another, finally ending up among the White Mountain Apaches, with whom she remained twelve years. Poston, the chronicler of Grijalva's life, relates that "about 1865 the White Mountain Indians made a treaty with the Americans at Fort Goodwin, when they brought Rosa into camp and Joe Palmer's wife hid Rosa under the bed until the Apaches had all gone. She afterward came to Bowie and from Bowie to Tucson, where she became an inmate of the family of Leopoldo Carrillo for two or three years, receiving a good deal of education and some training in the habits and customs of civilization." It was during that time that Marajildo and Rosa met. In 1867 they were married and settled upon the upper Gila, at Pueblo Viejo. Never having any children of their own, Rosa and Marajildo adopted Apache children—one boy and one girl.[8]

* * *

The literature bearing upon captives who have made their escape and endeavored to return to their former people would fill a small library; and names such as Inez Gonzales, Mickey Free, and Olive Oatman are all familiar. As their stories are all similar to the ones already presented, they have been purposely omitted. There does exist a host of cases which are difficult to assemble data on—of those captives who remained with Indians and became leaders and respected members of their tribes. In fact, some of the fiercest and most formidable fighters and chieftains came from the ranks of captives. Although looked upon as chattel by most Indian groups, many captives nevertheless became "well respected" and loved members of their tribe. The Apache Chief, Rafael, who laid waste to Sonora from 1800 to 1810, was of Opata descent; and allegedly was well educated by a Sonoran priest.[9] It is due to this training that Rafael was regarded as such a formidable foe. Being able to read and write he easily understood official dispatches. But what is even more important he had a deep knowledge of the traditions and habits of the Mexican people—all of which he utilized to full advantage.

As Grenville Goodwin pointed out, captives taken and adopted by the Western Apache came primarily from neighboring tribes, such as the Pima, Maricopa, Papago, Opata, and Navajos, as well as from Mexicans. All youths and grown men were killed during raiding, but children were brought home and either adopted, or placed in the captor's family as menials.[10] If young enough, these individuals underwent the same socialization process as any Apache child. Up to the age of seven or eight they received training from the squaws—and in the custom of the Apache, from the maternal side. With approach of puberty the youth was subjected to a hardening process and taught the ways of a warrior by his older and more experienced males. As happened in the case of Apache Bill and Marajildo Grijalva, Apache culture would thus be absorbed through a natural learning process.

Every frontiersman having anything to do with western tribes encountered these captives and soon learned what treacherous and savage combatants they could be. Peter R. Brady, chronicler to the A. B. Gray railroad survey in 1854, recalls meeting with a group of Coyotero Apaches near Calabasas. Among the Indians were two who acted as interpreters, whom Brady identifies as Mexicans, although they appeared to be "the most blood thirsty and treacherous rascals of them all." It was apparent to every member of the survey party that Apache socialization had eradicated every vestige of allegiance to their former people, when one captive informed the Anglos that they were going to attack Calabasas, and "kill all the Mexican men and take the women and children captives."[11]

Apache society and values offered the captive an easy transition from his former life to that of an Indian. As a Mexican he was limited by a rigid class structure —which allowed for little movement from one status level to another. If born a *pastore,* he would likely remain one for the rest of his life. The system of peonage, while classified as involuntary servitude, was so ensnaring that the individual never rose above it. Apache society offered male captives an opportunity to gain renown and prestige—as a warrior. The roles of male Apaches were oriented to warfare and the chase, and their education began at an early age. Captives entering the tribe fell naturally into the learning process. Although regarded as property by their captors, they nevertheless received the same strenuous training.

Close association with their Apache peers indelibly impressed upon their minds tribal tradition, values, and ethics—and if this continued uninterrupted over a period of years, it became impossible to distinguish the captives from the Indian.

If the captive was taken at an early, impressionable age, the process of socialization could indeed be rapid. Within the short span of a few years a Mexican child could undergo the Indianization process. Parents were often horrified to learn that the socialization process had broken the bonds of affection, and their child no longer evinced a desire to return to them. Such was the case with a Mexican family residing close to the Gardner ranch on the Sonoita River, southeast of Tucson, in the 1860s. During one foray, the Apaches abducted the son, then about six or seven years of age. For five years his father searched for the whereabouts of the child. When finally located the boy was in every respect an "Indian," and informed his father that "he was used to the Indians and wanted to stay with them."[12]

Often adoption of captives was motivated by the desire to replace a dead child or other relative, as well as to lessen the work load upon the Indian family or group. Among Apaches, as John Rope recounted, an aging tribesman would often be presented with a young captive to "lead you about when you get too old."[13] Ties of affection often developed in cases such as these, facilitating easy social integration of the captive into the kinship system, as well as orienting him to the values and social sanction of the group. As Hallowell points out, this was "functionally . . . equivalent to the normal processes of socialization in all societies, on which the psychological structuralization and personal adjustment of the human individual depends."[14] Little wonder therefore, that many Mexican and even Anglo captives refused to be liberated.

The process of adoption entailed the fullest kind of socialization, and it prepared the captive for every phase of Indian society. As has been alluded to, many of these "transculturites" rose to prominence within their tribes, usually on the merits of their prowess—as is the case of Gomez, the famed Mescalero whose war trails penetrated far into Mexico during the 1830s and 1840s. Most of these individuals married Indians, and not a few married captives, as did Rafael. From such unions came highly esteemed headmen. Such is the case of the saga of Cynthia Ann Parker, who was nine years of age when carried off by Comanches. For twenty-four years she resided among them, married a chief, Nokoni, and reared Quanah—the last great Comanche chief.[15]

Although Apaches and Comanches are accredited with holding the greatest number of captives, the Navajos also had their share. Raids upon Rio Grande settlements and against peripheral tribes furnished them with menials. As with the Apaches, integration of these individuals was governed by tribal social structure.

The social organization of the Navajos did not encourage slavery as it was commonly regarded during the period of the Civil War. While captives were considered chattel, for the most part they and their offspring were quickly absorbed into the tribe, thus losing their servile status. If a captive had been loyal for four years he could, according to Father Berard Haile,[16] ask for life of the deceased.[17]

During years that the captive served his abductor, his life was not his own. He was no more than personal property in the eyes of the Navajo, to be sold, or traded at will. Even his life could be taken at any time by his master. Value of a captive among the Navajos, as among other tribes, depended to a large extent on the difficulty encountered in obtaining him during the raid. War captives demanded higher values, and this is reflected in tribal prescribed methods of offering compensation. If friction arose between Navajos, and a member of one clan killed that of another, compensation was always demanded. In this case it was customary to dress a captive in robes and beads, set him upon a fine male horse, and present him in payment for the life of the deceased.[17]

If the captive served the term of servitude, and freedom was at last granted, he would be assigned a proper clan affiliation—*e.g.* Mexican (Nakhai), Ute (Noda'a), and Zuñi (Nanesht'ezhi). He was then at liberty to marry according to Navajo custom, acquire livestock, and in every sense of the word, become a functioning member within the framework of Navajo culture and society. It has been stated by observers of Indian ways and behavior,[18] that male captives enjoyed no process of amalgamation. They were always considered slaves and suffered every indignity. William Palmer claimed that many were emasculated, some had their tongues removed to prevent them from talking if recaptured, and others had their ears cut off to mark their servile status. There is no proof whatever of this kind of treatment of captives, on the part of the Navajo. On the contrary, statements of captives and their reluctance to accept freedom, points to just the opposite. The rapid return of Paiutes liberated by Agent Dennis Riordan, offers an excellent example, and speaks for the strength of ties between Navajos and their menials.

* * *

The process of transculturalization—as applied to captives—depends on a number of variables. Obviously, not all societies are equally receptive to assimilation of alien individuals. The fact that selective factors were at work, to ease the captive into his role and gradually "Indianize" him, became apparent when reminiscences, ethnohistory, and ethnology are consulted. The social organization of the receptor group must first be structured to afford integration. The clan system of southern Athapascan groups permitted rapid assimilation. There exists in both Apache and Navajo tribal structure a

198

number of "alien clans," which originated from the great influx of non-Athapascans entering the tribes since 1700, either as captives or refugees, fleeing Spanish vengeance.

The age at the time of abduction, as well as the length of residence of the captive were also selective factors. If taken at an early age, before socialization in their native society was completed, the individual easily fell into the ways and tradition of the tribe. Property concepts were another agent in determining whether or not the captive would be retained; and often mediated the type of treatment which he would receive. So too, did the value and ethical systems of both the Indian group and the original society contribute to the integration process. The attitude of various Indian groups toward captives decided the reasons behind abduction, and indeed, if the captive would be retained at all. The outlook of Anglo and Mexican society often decided the matter of returning to "freedom." An individual residing among Indians for any length of time was often hesitant to return to former "civilization." Often these ex-captives bore the marks of the red man—both physically, as in the case of Olive Oatman's tattoos; and psychological as in the aggressiveness of men like Apache Bill, and Grijalva.

* * *

1. A. Irving Hallowell, "American Indians, White and Black: The Phenomenon of Transculturalization," *Current Anthropology* (December 1963), p. 523.

2. John C. Cremony, *Life Among the Apaches* (San Francisco: 1868), p. 265.

3. Alan Le May, *The Searchers* (New York: Harper & Brothers, 1954); Will Cook, *Comanche Captives* (New York: Bantam Books, 1960).

4. S. M. Yost to J. L. Collins, January 14 and 18, 1859; New Mexico Superintendency Records, Letters Received from Agencies.

5. D. L. Hughes, Chapter in the Life of Apache Bill, mss. on

file at Arizona Pioneers' Historical Society, and the Special Collections Department, Library, University of Arizona, Tucson.

6. According to Sylvester Mowry, one-fourth of the Apaches in the early 1860s were Mexican captives or descendants. Sylvester Mowry, *Arizona and Sonora* (New York: Harper & Brothers, 1864), p. 31.

7. Hallowell, *op. cit.*, pp. 526-527.

8. Charles D. Poston, "The History of Marajildo and Rose Grijalva," Tucson *Weekly Star,* October 7, 1880.

9. *Putnam's Magazine* (Vol. IV, 1854), pp. 411-418.

10. Grenville Goodwin, *Social Organization of the Western Apache* (Chicago: University of Chicago Press, 1942), p. 96.

11. L. R. Bailey (ed.) *The A. B. Gray Report* (Los Angeles: Westernlore Press, 1963), pp. 204-206.

12. Reminiscence of Mary Gardner Kane, on file at the Arizona Pioneers' Historical Society.

13. Goodwin, *op. cit.,* p. 96.

14. Hallowell, *op. cit.,* pp. 526-527.

15. See Rupert N. Richardson, *The Comanche Barrier to South Plains Settlement* (Glendale: Arthur H. Clark Co., 1933), pp. 91-92.

16. Collection of Berard Haile, "Compensation for the Loss of a Clan Member," Special Collections, University of Arizona Library.

17. *Ibid.*

18. William R. Palmer, "Pahute Indian Government and Law," *Utah Historical Quarterly* (April 1929), p. 40.

APPENDIX
A PREAMBLE AND AN ACT FOR THE RELIEF OF INDIAN SLAVES AND PRISONERS

WHEREAS: By reason of the acquisition of Upper California and New Mexico, and the subsequent organization of the Territorial governments of New Mexico and Utah, by the acts of the Congress of the United States, these Territories have organized Governments within and upon what would otherwise be considered Indian territory, and which really is Indian territory so far as the right of soil is involved; thereby presenting the novel features of a white legalized government on Indian lands; and

WHEREAS: The laws of the United States in relation to intercourse with Indians are designed for, and only applicable to territories and countries under the sole and exclusive jurisdiction of the United States; and

WHEREAS: From time immemorial, the practice of purchasing Indian women and children, of the Utah tribe of Indians by Mexican traders, has been indulged in, and carried on by those respective people, until the

Indians consider it an allowable traffic, and frequently offer their prisoners or children for sale; and

WHEREAS: It is a common practice among these Indians to gamble away their own children and women; and it is well established fact, that women and children thus obtained, or obtained by war, or theft, or in any other manner, are by them frequently carried from place to place; packed upon horses and mules; larietted out to subsist upon grass, roots, or starve; and are frequently bound with thongs made of raw hide, until their hands and feet become swollen, mutilated, inflamed with pain, and wounded; and when with suffering, cold, hunger, and abuse they fall sick, so as to become troublesome, are frequently slain by their masters to get rid of them; and

WHEREAS: They do frequently kill their women and children taken prisoners, either in revenge, or for amusement, or through the influence of tradition, unless they are tempted to exchange them for trade, which they usually do if they have an opportunity; and

WHEREAS: One family frequently steals the children and women of another family; and such robberies and murders are continually committed, in times of their greatest peace and amity; thus dragging free Indian women and children into Mexican servitude and slavery, or death, to the almost entire extirpation of the whole Indian race; and

WHEREAS: These inhuman practices are being daily enacted before our eyes in the midst of the white settlements, and within the organized counties of the Territory; and when the inhabitants do not purchase or trade for those so offered for sale, they are generally doomed to the most miserable existence; suffering the tortures of every species of cruelty, until death kindly relieves them and closes the revolting scenery;

WHEREAS: When all these facts are taken into consideration, it becomes the duty of all humans and Christian people to extend unto this degraded and downtrodden race, such relief as can be awarded to them, according to their situation and circumstances; it therefore becomes necessary to consider;

FIRST: The circumstances of our location among these savage tribes under the authority of Congress, while yet the Indian title to the soil is left unextinguished; not even a treaty having been held, by which a partition of territory or country has been made, bringing them into our door-yards, our houses, and in contact with our every avocation.

SECOND: Their situation, and our duty towards them upon the common principles of humanity.

THIRD: The remedy or what will be the most conducive to ameliorate their condition, preserve their lives, and their liberties, and redeem them from a worse than African bondage; it suggests itself to your committee that to memorialize Congress to provide by some act of national legislation for the new and unparalleled situation of the inhabitants of this Territory, in relation to their intercourse with these Indians, would be one resource, prolific in its results for our mutual benefit; and further, that we ask their concurrence in the following enactment, passed by the Legislature of the Territory of Utah, January 31, A.D., 1852; entitled,

AN ACT FOR THE RELIEF OF INDIAN SLAVES AND PRISONERS

SEC. I: Be it enacted by the Governor and Legislative Assembly of the Territory of Utah: That whenever any white person within any organized county of this Territory, shall have any Indian prisoner, child or woman, in his possession, whether by purchase or otherwise; such person shall immediately go, together with such Indian prisoner, child or woman, before the select men or probate judge of the county. If in the opinion of the select men or probate judge the person having such Indian prisoner, child or woman, is a suitable person, and properly qualified to raise or retain and educate said Indian prisoner, child or woman; it shall be his or their duty to bind out the same, by indenture for the term not exceeding twenty years, at the discretion of the judge or select men.

SEC. II: The probate judge or select men shall cause to be written in the indenture, the name and age, place where born, name of parents if known, tribe to which said Indian person belonged, name of the person having him in possession, name of Indian from whom said person was obtained, date of the indenture; a copy of which shall be filed in the probate clerk's office.

SEC. III: The select men in their respective counties are hereby authorized to obtain such Indian prisoners, children or women, and bind them to some useful avocation.

SEC. IV: The master to whom the indenture is made is hereby required to send said apprentice to school, if there be a school in the district, or vicinity, for the term of three months in each year, at a time when said Indian child shall be between the ages of seven years and sixteen. The master shall clothe his apprentice in a comfortable and becoming manner, according to his, said master's condition in life.

NEW PUBLIC AFFAIRS BOOKS FROM TOWER

T-095-10   MORATORIUM: AN AMERICAN
           PROTEST   95¢
           by Paul Hoffman
           A top-flight political reporter examines the
           massive peace protests of 1969.

T-095-45   THE NEW NIXON   95¢
           by Paul Hoffman
           The author offers a tough, honest appraisal
           of the Nixon Administration—Vietnam, Cam-
           bodia, the "New Nixon" facade.

T-095-23   UP AGAINST THE WAR   95¢
           by Norma Sue Woodstone
           Controversial report of the young Americans
           opposed to the Vietnam War and the draft.
           Interviews with Movement leaders and ac-
           tivists.

T-095-18   WOMAN POWER: THE MOVEMENT
           FOR WOMEN'S LIBERATION   95¢
           by Cellestine Ware
           Fresh analysis of the resurgence of radical
           Feminism in America—the Movement is
           placed in historical perspective, and its present
           problems, constituencies, and prospects are ex-
           plored.

T-095-15   CRIME IN THE SUBURBS   95¢
           by David Loth
           An in-depth examination of why affluent sub-
           urban youth and adults turn to crime.

T-095-44   THE INFORMATION WAR   95¢
           by Dale Minor
           Highly controversial report on how the govern-
           ment *and* the press manipulate, censor, and dis-
           tort the news.

T-095-36   BARBARISM IN GREECE   95¢
           by James Becket
           A young American lawyer's shocking examina-
           tion of the use of torture by the military dicta-
           torship of Greece.

T-095-31   SKYJACK   95¢
           by Clark Whelton
           An explosive, original account of the recent
           airplane hijackings the world over . . . and
           the perplexing problems facing the airlines.

T-095-30   DRUGS AND THE YOUNG   95¢
           by John Garabedian
           An alarming report on the adolescent epidemic
           of drug abuse that is startling parents and kill-
           ing their children.

GHOST DANCE

MESSIAH

Paul Bailey

The true story of Wovoka, the Paiute Messiah, whose visions inspired the Indians to dreams of power, freedom, and peace but also led to bitter wars.

Tower   T-095-13   95¢

This is an original publication, not a reprint.

COMPACT HISTORY
OF THE
INDIAN WARS

John Tebbel

Fascinating account of the Indian Wars that raged in America for 300 years.

Tower   T-125-7 $1.25

TOWER'S exciting and popular

LASSITER Westerns
by Jack Slade